HEALING FIRE OF CHRIST

PAUL GLYNN

Healing Fire of Christ

Reflections on Modern Miracles—
Knock, Lourdes, Fatima

IGNATIUS PRESS　　SAN FRANCISCO

Original edition: *Healing Fire from Frozen Earth*
Published in 1999 by Marist Fathers Books,
Hunter's Hill, N.S.W., Australia
© 1999 by Fr. Paul Glynn
All rights reserved
New edition printed by permission of Fr. Paul Glynn, S.M.
The Society of Mary, Australia

Cover art: Nicolas Poussin, *Christ Healing the Blind at Jericho*,
The Louvre Museum, Paris
Reunion des Musées Nationaux / ArtResource, N.Y.
Cover design by Riz Boncan Marsella

Published in 2003 by Ignatius Press, San Francisco
All rights reserved
ISBN 0-89870-827-3
Library of Congress Control Number 00-109329
Printed in the United States of America ∞

Dedicated to Jack Josephs, 1925–1996,
man of God, good husband, father, grandfather, and friend,
helper of the poor,
serviceman in the Pacific War, and
thereafter worker for reconciliation, peace and love

CONTENTS

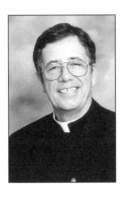

FOREWORD

As I was growing up, I wrestled with doubts about the existence of God and the kindness or "all-goodness" of this God. I presumed that I was not different from most young people trying to come to grips with the great questions of life. It was a great pleasure for me to be invited by Paul Glynn to write a foreword to his latest book, first because he is a good friend whom I admire very much, and second because I could resonate with so much that he has written about his own wrestling with the huge God questions.

This is a book that can keep you awake into the "wee small hours". I took the manuscript with me to a conference. I read each night till my eyes dropped out. Through his previous writings Paul Glynn has taught me so much about reconciliation and about the book of Psalms. Now he has reopened my mind and heart to the God who heals the broken, the wounded and the most wretched of the earth.

He writes of the many who think of suicide or give up trying in their marriage because of doubt, pain and loneliness. To help people who are thin on hope and peace of heart, Father Paul was not content just to do some reading research. He spent three months of 1997 at some of the famous healing shrines of the world in France, Poland, Portugal, England, Ireland and Mexico.

His research is thorough and detailed. He spoke at length with actual people who have been healed miraculously, to the extent that I feel I now know them personally. He met relatives, family, doctors and Church authorities. So conscientiously did he treat the material about which he was writing that, he admits, he would wake up in the middle of the night worried about the content of his writing. A psychiatrist friend comforted him by saying, "I'm glad to hear that! I'd be worried if you did not worry, since you are dealing with life-and-death matters for so many people."

I am quite sure, Paul Glynn, that your readers will find much enrichment from this book. People who claim to be agnostics or even atheists will certainly be challenged in their unbelief. Men and women of faith will have their faith strengthened. I can envision those in a state of confusion and depression being lifted up and given new direction. My final thought is that God, as found in your book, is "for real", and Mary is a genuinely caring, loving mother and friend.

Father Paul's previous books have been written to help seekers come closer to the heart of God. The books have sold very well, and all profits—to date, over half a million dollars—have gone to the impoverished of the Third World. A further $15,000 has gone to Saint Vincent de Paul work in Australia. All profits from the new book, *Healing Fire of Christ*, will likewise be channeled to the poor—those people, the Psalms assure us, who are so close to the heart of God.

+ Bishop David Cremin, D.D., E.V., V.G.
Hurstville, Sydney

INTRODUCTORY NOTES

For more than one thousand years before Christ, the Jews, his people, suffered war, invasions and persecutions. Many were forced to flee to other lands. One reason they held on to their faith and national identity was their practice of "going up" to Jerusalem on pilgrimage. Fifteen of the 150 Psalms begin with the title "Songs of Ascent". These were the Psalms sung on the occasion of pilgrimage back to Jerusalem. There were many roads to the Holy City, Zion, as it was called. Roads that came from Egypt, Ethiopia, Babylon, Syria, Greece or Rome. Paved roads, dirt roads, desert tracks. There are today many roads that lead to the outskirts of the New Jerusalem, which is belief in a loving God. This book is merely about one of these roads, a road that helped me on my way. Maybe it will help others.

I think it is normal if not almost universal for everyone at times to have difficulties in believing in a omnipotent, loving God, especially when things aren't going right. I had my biggest problems in my early twenties. It was not long after World War II. The newspapers and magazines carried horrendous stories and photos—Auschwitz, Dachau, Dresden, Nagasaki, prisoner of war camps. There were stories, too, of current degradation and barbarity in nations occupied by the Red Armies—Poland, Hungary, the Baltic States—and chilling rumors about slave labor camps and thought prisons in Siberia and parts of China. Was God no longer in control, or was he no longer? Was he ever?

I had some personal problems about *le bon Dieu*, the good God, even though I mostly repressed them. I will briefly recount them, as I think they had a bearing on my problems of faith. Maybe they will find an echo, even in the depths of the subconscious, of some readers who find it hard to believe.

My mother died when I was four years old. My only memory of her is her corpse. My fourteen-year-old sister Aileen lifted me up to the coffin so I could kiss my mother good-bye. I wondered why she didn't kiss me back, why her face was so cold. For years I feared that front room where the coffin had been placed and then suddenly disappeared. I would not go into it alone. I did not know the term then, but it was like a black hole in my little universe that was threatening to collapse in on itself.

After my mother's death something extraordinary happened. Her youngest sister, Molly, very close to our mother and us, took off her engagement ring and moved in with us children—we were seven, ranging from four years old to eighteen. She became a real mother to us, and we loved her deeply. Her ex-fiancé married someone else.

Tragedy struck again. For me, anyhow. I was eleven years old, and it was a Friday night in 1940, with my older siblings having left home or being away in boarding school. Aunty Molly gave me a very nice evening meal. After that, with a tense voice she said, "Tomorrow, your father is bringing home a new mother." The shock is still vivid in my memory.

She left our home early the next day, never to return. Dad arrived with his new wife, Lil, whom I'd never met before. She was a very good person and made my lonely father happy again. But to me she was an intruder. She had driven out Aunty Molly and the beautiful stories Aunty often told me of Nina Rose, my mother.

Our home was a devout Catholic one, and I did all the Christian things with everybody else. But seeds of doubt had been sown. If God loved me, why had he done these things to me? I remember my first Christmas holidays after we lost

Aunty Molly. The family was staying at Bondi Beach. It was a gloomy day, the sun losing out to heavy oppressive clouds that intermittently hurled down chill rainstorms. I sheltered in some rocks at one end of the beach, feeling quite desolate. I felt empathy with the seagulls calling mournfully to one another while dark waves crashed against the rocks below them. Such moments of loneliness can bring doubts about the goodness of life and of the Author of life. But they can bring something else, too. Dr. Anthony Storr, at the time professor of psychiatry at Oxford University, wrote of it in one of his books, *Solitude*: The experience of loneliness, with the sense of alienation it often brings, can be a wonderful catalyst to help us look deeper and "find meaning in the universe . . . beyond fashionable things".

My doubts about an omnipotent Creator who cared for me personally had gradually led to doubts about the Bible, above all, the Gospels. The story that charms children at Christmas, of God becoming man, and about this Jesus walking the roads of Judea and Galilee forgiving sins and healing sicknesses, dying a martyr of love but rising from the tomb and promising eternal life to us—this is all very beautiful. But is it true? It happened two thousand years ago. Maybe it is just a combination of yearnings, spun by compassionate souls wanting to lessen grief and fear in human hearts—like the bedtime fairy stories told to crying children. However, if the Gospel stories about instantaneous healing of physical ills like leprosy and blindness were true, then the supernatural was real, more real than our transient little human securities and joys. If the healing stories and the Resurrection were true, the gospel really would be good news giving meaning and beauty even to lives burdened with toil, drudgery and pain. I wanted to believe the latter, yet how could I be sure? I felt I was in one of those gray dreams where the power to act leaves your legs and arms.

I had heard extraordinary claims about healings at Lourdes. I decided to investigate them and began reading as many books as I could lay my hands on. As I read the accounts, I tried conscientiously to find loopholes in the stories, weak links in the testimonies, inconsistencies or possible natural explanations of the cures. I gradually came to think the stories seemed to be unassailable facts.

I read some books at the time about philosophers arguing that we cannot be certain of anything but our own thoughts: Could we be creating the apparent realities around us, our bodies included, just as we create people, incidents and even new selves when we dream during sleep? I decided no, despite such theories being proposed by some university professors; this kind of all-embracing doubt was against common sense and was obviously false. I really exist, every part of me, and so do my family and friends. Our minds can know truth; our senses and our common sense do put us in touch with reality.

My gradually formed conviction that instantaneous healing of verified physical diseases like cancer and tuberculosis was happening at Lourdes meant for me that God and his Christ are real, that they do listen to prayer and show loving care to us mortals. One of the messages to Bernadette Soubirous, the Lourdes seer, is that our mortal lives are essentially a journey, not a terminus. Life is sometimes painful, like most long journeys are, but its destination is sharing in God's full life of love forever. This makes all the wear, tear and pain of the journey eminently worthwhile.

This present era we inhabit is surely as out of joint as the immediate post–World War II era that disturbed many of us in youth. The newscasts are saturated with violence—ethnic cleansing in the Balkans, genocide in Africa, deaths by drug overdose, aboriginal stories of stolen childhoods, a high divorce rate with legacies of those stolen childhoods, suicide as the number-one killer of Australians between fifteen and twenty-four years of age. . . .

Many commit suicide or give up trying in their marriage because they find no meaning but only doubt, pain and loneliness. In the hope of helping some hurting people who have become thin on hope and peace of heart, I am writing this book. For preparation, I spent three months of 1997 at healing shrines—Lourdes and Rue du Bac in France, Fatima in Portugal, Czestochowa in Poland, Walsingham in England, Knock in Ireland and Guadalupe in Mexico. I found in these places a strong sense of community and compassion and received great cooperation from those in charge. I brought back to Australia much research material to add to some excellent books on these places in Sydney libraries. I have planned the book for people in the street searching for what is true and good but who, because of their personal responsibilities, do not have time and wherewithal to do in-depth research.

Several years ago I read a sentence written by a Greek monk who died in Cellia, Egypt, in 399. This Evagrius of Pontus had a profound influence on the Christian spirituality of his day and beyond. His sentence, which contains wise direction and also a sharp warning, is this: "A good theologian is one whose prayer is true." If you want to know and teach others about God and the supernatural, you had better be a good pray-er.

Augustine also profoundly affected Christian thinking in his fourth- to fifth-century lifetime and down to the present. He once wrote of people who take great strides, but in the wrong direction! He also warned of unreflecting people who rush headlong into a spiritual oasis but end up muddying the waters, for themselves and for others. I knew I must do a lot of praying if my proposed book was to be of any real help to anyone.

I told a psychiatrist friend that in the course of writing this book I often woke from sleep in the small hours, worried about what I was writing. He said, "Good, I am glad to hear that. I'd be worried if you didn't worry! You are writing about difficult and profoundly important matters. They are literally life-or-death matters to many people, many who are in distress. I presume you would not attempt writing a book about God, belief and our supernatural destinies in a carefree, shallow or heedless way." His words comforted me—above all because he is a wise and loving man, very dedicated to helping the long lines of his clients.

Like that funny little boy who sometimes leans his round head on a tree and sighs "Good grief!" I am far from having it all together. Like Charlie Brown I still get my kites tangled in the limbs of trees, drop baseball catches and have many a Lucy glare at me deservedly. But if what I write is true, if God is real and loves each one of us, if life is a journey meant to lead home to him, then our tangled kites, dropped catches and criticisms from Lucy are not such a big deal. Dr. Viktor Frankl, graduate of Auschwitz, used to say: You can put up will all kinds of pain if you have a logos, a reason for living. He also said, "Don't invent a meaning for your life. It is there. Find it."

Jacques Maritain was one of the great minds of the twentieth century. He wrote more than sixty books that were widely read—books on philosophy, art, sociology, politics and, above all, finding God. He had lost the vague Christian faith of his childhood by the time he was studying in the science department of the Sorbonne University. He met a young woman in the same course, Raïssa Oumansoff. She was a Russian Jew who had fled to France with her family to escape the anti-Semitism of the land of her birth. She, too, had lost her childhood belief in God. At that time the professors in the Sorbonne science department were openly dedicated to the belief that "science alone can provide answers to what torments modern minds and hearts". Young Jacques and Raïssa were left deeply dissatisfied and often discussed their future, and Europe's, ominously. They fell in love but wondered out loud if it was right to bring children into a world that seemed to be so painful in its chaos and meaninglessness. They decided to attend the lectures of Henri Bergson, who was leading an intellectual reaction against the current worship of science. He encouraged them to look for something deeper, even an Absolute.

They married in 1904 and then met Léon Bloy, the French novelist. He had rediscovered Christ as a young man and helped them in their quest to put a heart and face and personal name to the Absolute that Bergson spoke of. In 1906 the Maritains were baptized. They worked together for almost sixty years, writing books together or singly. They warned Europe of what would follow from its unquestioning belief in science and materialistic progress. The two world wars proved them prophetic.

Jacques Maritain wrote: "Having given up God so as to be self-sufficient, man has lost track of his soul. He looks in vain for himself; he turns the universe upside down trying to find himself. He finds masks, and behind masks, death." Isn't this like our modern society, described by Pope John Paul II as "the culture of death"?

But I am becoming too academic. We have had so many "saving" theories and ideologies since the eighteenth-century Enlightenment that moderns, especially the younger generation, are wary of them! They have seen such massive and often destructive conning by peddlers of ideologies. However, moderns seem to like hearing true stories about real people. That is why this book is mainly a series of people's experiences of instantaneous physical healing. In the first section of the book are the people I met personally. The others are equally real, discovered especially in the signed documents and testimonies found in the archives of the Lourdes Medical Bureau. Since Dr. de Saint Maclou began the bureau in 1885, doctors there have carefully collected and filed scientific data on some thousands of cures that are medically inexplicable. This will be taken up in detail in a later chapter. For me and many others these cures are proof of what Jesus said in John 5:17: "My Father goes on working and so do I." John's Gospel uses the word "sign" in preference to "miracle" when dealing with Jesus curing the sick. A sign is not a proof, much less a destination. It signifies a road. Whether you call them signs or miracles, they cannot "coerce" belief, as Cardinal Newman and so many other great believers have said. Belief is a choice of the will, like love. Signs are not overpoweringly self-evident to the mind as is a mathematical truth like $2 + 2 = 4$. Everyone has the ability to reject belief, or love or conscience or all kinds of moral evidence. As will be pointed out in a separate chapter, Alexis Carrel, who was to be awarded the Nobel Prize for medicine, witnessed several instantaneous healings of serious physical illnesses at Lourdes. He even wrote a book about one of these cases, showing it was medically inexplicable. However, he did not immediately come to accept Lourdes miracles as the direct action of the loving Creator. For a number of years he reached no conclusion, remaining in what has been termed the "comfortable, nondemanding territory of agnosticism". But then he began to pray and received from God the gift of faith. In an April 1941 *Reader's Digest* article, he spoke of the "tranquility... greater intellectual vigor, moral stamina, and a deeper understanding of realities underlying human relationships" that prayer brings. "We derive most power from prayer", his article continued, "when we use it, not as a petition, but as a supplication that we may become more like him." That, he had come to see, is real prayer.

I am writing this book for one purpose only: To help people on the journey to discover God and/or to come closer to him in love. If such a journey of discovery appeals to you, I hope you will add prayer as an accompaniment to reading this book. You can pray before you are convinced a loving God exists. Dr. Takashi Nagai, the hero of the Nagasaki A-bomb, had been a convinced atheist. Impressed by Blaise Pascal's *Pensées* and by some Japanese Christians he met, he began praying as a kind of experiment, not unlike his experiments in the lab of the Nagasaki Medical University. He said prayer and study brought him into God's sustaining presence. Concerning the horrendous days following the dropping of the atomic bomb, he wrote, "God walked with us survivors through the nuclear desert of Nagasaki." That experience of a God who did not so much explain the sufferings of the A-bomb victims as share in them gave Dr. Nagai tremendous courage, strength and serenity. People came from all over Japan, then going through its post–Pacific War "dark valley", to consult this "holy man of Nagasaki", living in a tiny hut built over the place where he had found the charred remains of his beloved wife, Midori. His deep love and his serenity gave them a feeling of hope and peace. He also spoke of his own Lourdes miracle, when in a medically inexplicable way he was instantaneously healed of fatal A-bomb wounds on September 8, 1945. It was the day on which Mary of Nazareth's birthday is commemorated. His mother-in-law simply made the sign of the cross on Takashi Nagai's lips with water from the Lourdes shrine built in Nagasaki by Maximilian Kolbe.

Chapter 1

MARIE KERSLAKE

And Dr. West's Bitter Pills

HILAIRE BELLOC, a man with "fire in his belly", wrote books and poems that stirred people and still do. He was brought up a Catholic, but his faith in the Gospels underwent a crisis in 1893, when he began classical studies at Balliol College, Oxford University. He felt the pull of agnosticism and "the intellectual pleasures of scepticism". He lost his faith for a while, which gave him a sympathy for agnostics in his later public controversies about religion. He had returned to belief by 1902, when his highly acclaimed book *The Path to Rome* was published. In a preface he wrote in 1914 for Johannes Jorgensen's *Lourdes*, he spoke of a momentous discovery he made "about Easter time, 1904 . . . that at Lourdes the best influence there is for us, Our Lady, is active". Alluding to the popular newspaper dismissal of Lourdes miracles as "merely the result of heightened emotion of uneducated, unsophisticated people", he challenged doubters "to go to

Lourdes and study the physical cures that take place". He concluded in this preface, "It is the greatest experience they are likely to have in the modern world." Many an atheist, agnostic or lapsed Catholic who has regained faith in the Christ of the Gospels at Lourdes finds no hyperbole in that last sentence.

Belloc and his wife, Elodie, took their children to Lourdes. Sixteen-year-old Eleanor witnessed an actual miracle of healing. That, and her subsequent reading about Lourdes, made so profound an impression that some years later she talked her non-Catholic husband, Reginald Jebb, into spending their honeymoon there! One of their sons, Philip, became a Bene- dictine monk at Downside Abbey, near Bath, England, and was prior when I was there in August 1997. "You're research- ing miracles?" he said to me. "Then go down the road a few miles and meet Marie Kerslake." I did so, in the company of internationally known theologian Sebastian Moore, O.S.B., also of Downside Abbey.

Marie Kerslake lives in Frome, Somerset, and I found her friendly and unmelodramatic but very ready to tell her story. She has an attractive sense of humor—which she had sorely needed some years earlier. She had been an active woman, happy wife and mother of seven children, and a keen tennis and golf player, until disaster struck in 1962. Her joints began to pain and stiffen. Dr. J. D. Corcoran, the family doctor, diagnosed rheumatoid arthritis and tried the best current treatment. She became worse, and he sent her to a specialist, Dr. Cosh, at the Royal National Hospital for Rheumatic Diseases, in nearby Bath. Dr. Cosh diagnosed osteoarthritis and began specialized treatment, a variety of oral medications and, on several occasions, steroid injections into the joints. However, her pain, stiffness and immobility increased.

In 1977 Marie had a heart attack. Dr. Corcoran had her admitted to Guy's Hospital Heart Unit. The ECG showed

Dom Sebastian Moore and Marie Kerslake, August 1997.

extensive damage, and Dr. Corcoran said the heart specialist gave him "a very pessimistic report about her future. . . . Two months later she was having a lot of central chest pain."

From her son who attended Downside School, attached to the monastery, Marie heard of a Lourdes pilgrimage being organized by Dom Philip Jebb, Belloc's grandson. The monks, with the help of Downside Old Boys, had set up a group that ran a daily soup kitchen for down-and-outs in London and summer camps for handicapped children. They also took pilgrimages of the sick to Lourdes. They transported the latter in "jumbulances", motor vehicles with twelve beds and enough space for twenty-eight volunteer helpers.

Marie set out in one of the jumbulances on the July 1978 pilgrimage. Dr. Corcoran said she was now "a very sorry picture. . . . Her condition, in the normal course of events, would have left her completely incapacitated by 1979. She was confined to a wheelchair and severely troubled by pain in her joints, spine and neck and forced to wear a surgical collar." Traveling with her was Tom Clifford, now Lord Clifford, a descendant of aristocrats who had remained Catholic during England's penal times. A graduate of Downside, he had lost 90 percent of his vision in a car crash. He became a team with Marie, helping her with her wheelchair while she became their eyes.

They arrived at Lourdes, and, Marie told me, she did not offer a single prayer for her own cure. Her attention was riveted on two fellow pilgrims, Peggy Hicks, a nurse who was suffering from motor-neuron disease, and Monica, in the last stages of cancer, who was to die at Lourdes.

As the Masses, processions and prayers can be quite tiring for the very sick, Dom Philip decided after several days to take the group on an outing in the beautiful Pyrenees Mountains immediately south of Lourdes. They stopped in

Dom Philip Jebb.

Gavarnie for Mass at a chapel built by the Knights of Malta for pilgrims walking from France to Compostella in Spain. Marie noted with admiration the signboard outside the chapel reading: "Compostella 911 km". It was July 26, 1978, a day indelibly imprinted on her memory.

Mass began with Marie in her wheelchair and Tom Clifford close by. Then came the elevation of the Host. Without being conscious of what she was doing, Marie got out of the chair, knelt down and bowed in adoration. Clifford could vaguely see she had left her chair and begged her to desist. "But I just had to kneel," she told me later,

and after Mass I got up and said, "Tom, I don't know if you realize it: I'm walking! I can walk!" We left the chapel in tandem, and outside I realized my finger joints were no longer useless. Just for the sheer joy of it, I began pulling up grass from the roadside, reveling in the mobility and feeling in my hands.

I returned to the chapel and said to Father Philip, "Look, I can walk properly." Until now when I walked I had to lean on two sticks and progress along by swiveling my legs and stiff knees one at a time. He was worried I might do damage to myself by suddenly abandoning sticks and wheelchair. I had come as a crippled pilgrim without my husband or family, and he was responsible for my welfare. He feared I was forcing myself to walk and asked me to get back into the wheelchair. I did so, and we continued our outing in the bus.

Before the evening procession, I told Father Philip I wanted to walk in it. He repeated that I might do myself harm, so I went in the wheelchair. But my whole body told me otherwise. After the procession I went to the Grotto in my wheelchair and spent a long time thanking our Lady for my cure.

It was very late when I finished my prayer and returned to the hotel. Father Philip was on the lookout for me, worried. I saw him, jumped out of the wheelchair and ran to greet him. When he saw me running, his doubts dissolved, and he broke into tears. So did I. I ceremoniously discarded my surgical collar and my sticks and pushed the wheelchair away. Rejoicing broke out among the pilgrims still up. I seized one of them and began to dance.

That was late Wednesday night. On Friday, July 28, I was taken to the Medical Bureau, with Dom Stephen Worth, O.S.B., to translate my words into French. The president, Dr. Théodore Mangiapan, gave me a scolding for letting a day go by without reporting the possible cure. Our pilgrimage doctor then explained my medical state just two days ago. Dr. Mangiapan took down the details, said my case was "worth investigating" and asked me to return in a year's time if my "cure" continued. I was to bring a full report of my previous ailments, signed by the doctors who treated me, and their assessment of my medical condition over the coming twelve months.

I returned home, very happy to be well and able to take up knitting, weaving and tennis again. My poor husband found it all quite bewildering! For the last five years he had had to do almost everything for me. Now I was as able as he! He just couldn't grasp the change!

My doctors were delighted and cooperated 100 percent with the requests of Dr. Mangiapan. All the old reports and X rays were gathered from the Royal National Hospital for Rheumatic Diseases. The doctors were so intrigued by the change in me that they refused payment on a new set of X rays.

One section of Dr. Corcoran's report reads, "Before going to Lourdes, she was in a partially crippled condition, unable to get around the house. She had been unable to walk up the short hill outside her home in Norton Saint Philip. Now she is an extremely active woman and can run up the same hill. She is more remarkably improved than anyone in my experience. Before she went to Lourdes," he added, "the specialist who monitored her after her heart attack was pessimistic about how long she would survive."

Marie described the events that occurred twelve months after her cure.

One year later I presented myself at the Lourdes Medical Bureau, having sent on ahead my hospital reports and X rays. I was in for a shock! Fourteen doctors who had read the reports gathered around me like devil's advocates. They told me to strip. I looked around for a changing room. "Right where you are", they said! Most spoke English and proceeded to handle my arms and legs to see how well the joints worked. They peppered me with questions, seemingly trying to find loopholes in my testimony. One doctor in particular upset me badly by his hostile cross-examining. As I told the Bath newspaper that interviewed me some time later, he was more like the KGB interrogating a suspected spy! This grueling examination went on for three and one-half hours straight. They staggered me at its merciful conclusion by telling me to report back for more at 5:30 P.M.!

I returned to the Medical Bureau to find their number had swelled to twenty-five doctors. Once again I was poked, weighed, measured and had limbs pushed and bent to ascertain suppleness. My bodily coordination and even my eyes were tested. This second examination lasted two and one-half hours. At the conclusion they told me to come back in a year's time, bringing progress reports again from Dr. Corcoran.

I went home rather upset by the attitude of one doctor in particular, who seemed to doubt everything about my cure. Some time later I was watching a British television panel discussion on miracles. My attention was suddenly riveted on that *bête noire* doctor, right there on the panel! Asked if he had ever seen what he considered a true miraculous healing, he said yes. He proceeded to detail my case. My resentment against him vanished—he had questioned me like that to get medical certitude. A devil's advocate in God's service!

The Marie Kerslake case was well described in the book *Lourdes: A Modern Pilgrimage*, by Patrick Marnham.[1] No one could call Marnham pious in his approach. He seemed to take

[1] Patrick Marnham, *Lourdes: A Modern Pilgrimage* (New York: Coward, McCann and Geoghegan, 1981).

Marie Kerslake arriving at Lourdes, July 1978.

delight in pointing out all the oddities of Lourdes. The sale of "pious souvenirs" especially annoyed him. However, he did portray the essential Lourdes factually and presented some of the famous miracles, finding them inexplicable if one denies the supernatural. His background probably has made Marnham cynical and therefore an ideal devil's advocate to sniff out the unauthentic. First he graduated in law at Corpus Christi College, Oxford, and was called to the bar. Experience tends to make lawyers suspicious! Then, having established himself as a writer with his book *The Road to Katmandu*, he was launched on a second career as a journalist—writing regular articles for the *Spectator, Books for Bookworms* and the *Daily Telegraph*. Journalists have to watch their backs if they write on controversial topics like the supernatural!

Marnham gave five pages to Marie Kerslake's cure, having met her and her doctor, Dr. Corcoran. He also quoted an attack on the miraculous nature of her cure by a Dr. D. J. West in his dismissive book *Eleven Lourdes Miracles*.[2] West's book, funded by the New York Parapsychology Foundation, attacked the examinations by the Lourdes Medical Bureau (including that of Marie Kerslake) as unscientific and therefore unreliable. Marnham asked Dr. David Morrell, professor of general practice at Saint Thomas' Hospital, London, to read Dr. West's dismissal of Lourdes cures as simply cures of "hysteria" via religious emotionalism. Professor Morrell found Dr. West's explanations almost as remarkable as miraculous cures! Patients suddenly recovering from very organic conditions, such as vomiting blood, discharging pus from abdominal walls, suffering prolonged incontinence, paralysis or blindness—all observed over a period by their own doctors—can hardly be dismissed as cases of "mere hysteria", he wrote. He found Dr. West's criticisms to be unscientific and lacking in common sense.

Dom Philip Jebb also has no doubt that the woman Marie Kerslake whom he escorted to Lourdes was not suffering from "mere hysteria". He has seen the original medical reports from her doctors, who live not far from Downside Abbey. He witnessed the instantaneous remission, though he first feared it might only be temporary, and he has observed her vigorous health for more than nineteen years since. He also knows she is a person of plain common sense, not given to flights of fancy, neurotic or otherwise.

Many people who are healed at Lourdes cannot afford to keep returning for yearly Medical Bureau examinations. On his second pilgrimage as a stretcher bearer (*brancardier*), Dom Philip told me, he helped a Scot, Jim McSorley, who was paralyzed from the neck down. He remembered him especially because he found it so difficult to catch the thick

[2] D. J. West, *Eleven Lourdes Miracles* (London: Gerald Duckworth, 1957).

Scottish accent. Two hours after helping McSorley into the baths, he saw the same man in Seven Dolours Hospital sitting up in bed and cutting up his own meal—surrounded by very excited people. There are many Jim McSorleys who are not on the books because they are not in a position to return each year for half a dozen years and more for Medical Bureau checks.

If, as Dr. West argued, it's all just natural, just a curing of hysteria, why are thousands of extraordinary cases of instantaneous healing documented at Lourdes and not elsewhere? Why don't we see extraordinarily detailed reports of cures like Marie Kerslake's being issued by psychiatrists' associations? There are numerous psychiatrists and doctors in the world dealing with millions of patients each year.

The Lourdes doctors risk their reputations by going public. What do they gain? Cynicism and sarcasm, sometimes, from the Dr. Wests, but certainly no money They work as volunteers in the service of God or sometimes just of the truth. Some who sign the examinations are agnostics or atheists. They are honest enough to sign statements of what they have seen without understanding anything about causes of the remarkable recoveries.

You may have read about the Soviet encyclopedias written by Russian professors when Communist ideology dictated what must be written. To the astonishment of the Western academic world, Russians were accredited with all kinds of scientific breakthroughs. Something similarly "rigged" happens, it seems to me, with some of the attacks by academics on Lourdes miracles. If you begin with the unscientific (because unproven) ideology that supernatural miracles cannot happen, you must deny Lourdes miracles.

Professor Morrell challenged Dr. West to come up with evidence of any other places where remissions of blindness, tuberculosis or malignancies happen instantaneously as at

Lourdes. West's explanations, wrote Morrell, "stretch the reader's credibility". West wrote that the great majority of cures concern potentially recoverable conditions and are "remarkable only for the speed and manner in which they are said to have taken place". But that's the very point: Instantaneous remission! Where are such instantaneous remissions happening in the medical practice of doctors in the many hospitals and clinics around the world? In 1734 Pope Benedict XIV—called "the scholars' pope"—set down seven conditions for the acceptance of a cure as miraculous. He was writing about miracles studied for the beatification and canonization of reputed "saints". One of the seven conditions is that the disease cured must have been an organic one (such as observable cancer) and not just a psychological one (such as depression). The fourth condition is "that the cure was sudden—instantaneous".

Protestant writer Ruth Cranston, in her classic *The Miracle of Lourdes*,[3] devoted many pages to instantaneous cures of very physical diseases. She understood that "instantaneousness" is of the essence of Lourdes' cures. She presented this as evidence for the existence of God—and a modern corroboration of the miracles of Christ in the Gospels. For Cranston the healing of doubts about the meaning and worth of human existence was more important than the healing of bodies at Lourdes.

Dom Sebastian Moore was silent for a time as he drove me away from the Marie Kerslake interview. I was happy to be quiet, content to gaze through the car window at the beauty of the Somerset fields bordering the country road. The silent countryside spoke to me, as Marie's healing did, of the triumph of God's goodness and the worthwhileness of life. Suddenly Dom Sebastian spoke.

[3] Ruth Cranston, *The Miracle of Lourdes*, updated ed. (New York: Image Books, 1988).

"That was a moving experience!" he said. "But isn't it sad, even awesome, that disbelieving and denying the supernatural has become the norm for moderns! Fascinated by all the failures in human history, past and present, people say, 'There you are: the failures prove that God, Christ and the Christian Church can't be valid, can't be real! Unbelievers unite, throw off the chains of miracles and religious faith, drive out the believers!' What a contrast to the simple, hopeful, joyful experience Marie Kerslake had!"

Marie Kerslake's cure took place at Gavarnie, which is some miles outside Lourdes, farther south in the Pyrenees Mountains. For this reason the cure will not be accepted by the Lourdes Medical Bureau as one of its own. The bureau spends a huge number of hours checking and rechecking each reported cure. This is repeated yearly for five years and more. The Medical Bureau has no shortage of actual Lourdes cures to investigate. It has now adopted a rule not to accept as belonging to Lourdes cures taking place elsewhere, such as this Gavarnie case.

Marie Kerslake,
one year after her cure,
back at Lourdes (with
pilgrimage bus driver).

Chapter 2

MARION CARROLL

Knock, Sunday, September 3, 1989

AUGUSTINE SAID God is working miracles all the time—if we look at the wonders of nature, or our own bodies or just our eyes, we discover myriads of miracles. Unfortunately, we tend to lose our sense of wonder. So every so often, Augustine said, God works a miracle in an extraordinary, startling way. Miracle cures are startling and encouraging, as is meeting the recipients. I have discovered there are a joyfulness and freshness to these people, a simplicity and a humility. I found these qualities when I met Marion Carroll in Athlone, seventy-five miles west of Dublin.

She was born Marion McCormack in 1951 in this city on the Shannon River, also birthplace of the tenor Count John McCormack (no relation). Her parents were not well off. While she was a tiny child, they were forced to make ends meet by going off to work in England, leaving her with relatives. Tuberculosis was a dreaded killer among Ireland's poor in the 1950s. Marion contracted it when she was only seven years old. She was sent to the Peamount Sanatorium, Dublin, and the doctors warned her family that her life was in grave danger. Her father, who often used to read his children the lives of the saints, led the family in prayers to Mary. The little one survived, and, despite his meager resources, he had a Lourdes Grotto built in Athlone to thank the Mother of God, convinced Mary's prayers to God had saved Marion's life. The child developed a special prayer bond with Mary.

Marion was no lover of schoolbooks. When she finished compulsory education at age fourteen, she left school and waltzed casually through her remaining teen years as factory worker, shop assistant and waitress. She lost her heart to Elvis Presley's songs, and her mother wondered if his pictures might displace the images of the Sacred Heart and Mary on her bedroom walls. But they did not.

Then came a redheaded Irish soldier who put Elvis right out of her mind. She met Jimmy Carroll at a dance in December 1970 and fell in love "truly, madly, deeply".

An Irish soldier's pay wasn't much in those days, so Jimmy had to work hard at getting enough money to rent a house. Then he asked McCormack if he could marry his daughter. Marion's joy was dissipated soon after the wedding, however, when Jimmy was sent on a tour of duty with the United Nations peacekeepers in Cyprus.

Their first child, Anthony, was born in 1973, and soon after that Marion's problems started. She took little notice at first, having heard of many mothers having postnatal problems. On top of a great tiredness, she was getting a sensation of pins and needles in one leg as well as bouts of intense pain. When Anthony was ten months old she moved toward his crib one day and suddenly found herself falling onto it. The doctor diagnosed a slipped disc and put her leg in traction for some weeks. There was no improvement, and her chronic tiredness grew in intensity. She began having temporary blackouts. When a sharp-tongued relative dismissed her complaints as just "nerves and malingering", Marion decided to keep her troubles to herself. Nor did she tell Jimmy, who was away in the army.

By the time Cora was born in late 1976, Marion was often unsteady on her feet and with her grip. She only cuddled Cora by laying her on the double bed, lest she drop her. She had given birth to both children by cesarean and began to suspect that this had caused her physical debility and increasing sense of being a wrung-out rag. She suffered frequent headaches, and her vision began to swim.

At Jimmy's father's funeral, Marion had a complete blackout and fell to the ground. They rushed her to Tullamore Hospital. When she opened her eyes, everything was blurred, and colors were jumbled together. Her hearing was very faint. The doctor suggested she go to Dublin for a brain scan and also to have a kidney infection looked at. It was 1978.

After Marion had been hospitalized several days and examined by a neurologist, Jimmy was suddenly called from his barracks in Cork to the hospital. The neurologist wanted him to break the news to Marion. Jimmy wrote the dreaded words on his hand with a ballpoint pen. As soon as he came to her bedside, she knew something was wrong. Jimmy was not due for leave. He dismissed her worries, but she noticed writing on his hand. Maybe he subconsciously glanced at it. As he tried to draw his hand away, she held it and read MULTIPLE SCLEROSIS.

Irish author John Scally wrote a book, *Marion: A Modern-Day Miracle*, in which he detailed Marion's steady decline over the years from 1978, when she was told she had multiple sclerosis (MS), until her cure at Knock in 1989.[1] It makes for

---

[1] John Scally, *Marion: A Modern-Day Miracle* (Dublin: Basement Press, 1995).

sad reading, telling how her body deteriorated and she got around shakily on two sticks. Jimmy had a simple but rock-solid faith in Christ's teaching and in the meaning of the marriage vows. He nursed Marion at home, took her on regular trips to the hospital and specialists and encouraged her with the latters' hopes of "the latest American breakthrough". When her hand shook too much to hold a cup of tea, he gave her straws.

In 1983 the Carrolls moved back to Athlone, and Dr. Patrick O'Meara took over her case. He boosted her morale and Jimmy's tremendously by excellent medical help and deeply spiritual values. In 1988 pain and debility increased in Marion's legs, and she had some bad falls. Dr. O'Meara put her into Athlone Hospital. From now on, he said, she was to be permanently in a bed or wheelchair. Her kidney infection had flared up again, her speech was slurring badly, and her throat muscles were gradually contracting. She could no longer hold up her head, so in August 1989 Dr. O'Meara put her into a surgical collar. She was now doubly incontinent. "I was at a stage where I had no dignity left", she said. "MS had taken that." At this stage she had to be strapped into her wheelchair or she could fall out. She had lost use of both legs, was blind in the right eye and had partial sight in the left. As she lost strength in her bite and her throat muscles deteriorated, all food given to her had to be liquefied so she could sip through a straw. Dr. O'Meara was treating her for kidney and thyroid problems and for a hiatus hernia.

Jimmy's devotion and the family Rosary were rays in her darkness, Marion said. The car Jimmy had proudly bought several years earlier had to be sold to pay medical bills. Jimmy would push her to Mass in her wheelchair, one and one-half miles each way.

Marion had a great longing to go to Lourdes, but the family's precarious finances ruled that out. At the beginning

Mrs. Judy Coyne of the Knock Shrine Handmaids, August 1997.

of September their friend Gerry Glynn, a local ambulance driver, called in and said he was free on Sunday, September 3. How about it if he drove her to Knock in his ambulance? She said no; she did not feel up to a sixty-mile journey. Besides, Dr. O'Meara had told her to be ready for a major kidney operation the following week. But Jimmy and Gerry said the trip to Knock would help her. They argued strongly, and, against her better judgment, she agreed. She felt she would soon be dead, anyhow.

Gerry strapped her onto the bed in his ambulance, put the folded wheelchair aboard and set off. Because of her state, he drove cautiously. The driving took much more out of her than Jimmy and Gerry had anticipated. Marion told me that, being incontinent, she was all "messed up" by the time they reached Knock. Judy Coyne—founder and head of the Knock Handmaids—told me she personally helped clean Marion. "Do you remember Marion Carroll?" I asked her in 1997. "Remember her? How could I forget her?" she said. "The ambulance driver brought her to our station because she was in a terrible state. As I cleaned her up, I discovered her legs were paralyzed, and she had no power in her hands. She was quite blind in one eye. The other was blurred. Her words were jumbled and almost unintelligible. I've seen many sick and dying here in Knock. I had serious doubts about this one making it back to Athlone alive!"

Judy Coyne, still quite a force despite her age, ordered the cleaned-up Marion to rest at the Handmaids Centre until the ceremonies began. Then they pushed her, strapped tight in her wheelchair, into the Basilica and right up directly in front of the statue of Mary of Knock.

Marion continued the story: "I looked up and thought the statue was the most beautiful and friendly I had ever seen. I knew I was dying, and my children needed a mother. Above

Shrine of Knock, Ireland.

all I was sad for Jimmy. We had been married seventeen years, and most of that time he was burdened with a sick wife. I couldn't get my thoughts in order. I wanted to try to express them to another woman, another housewife who would understand. So I looked up at our Lady and said: 'You are a mother, too. You know how I feel about leaving my husband and children.' It wasn't a prayer; it wasn't a statement; it was just one woman chatting to another. I then prayed to her asking her to look after Jimmy and the children and give them the grace to accept my death as the will of God."

Bishop Colin O'Reilly concluded the Rosary and prayers for the sick. He led a team of priests anointing the sick, including Marion. She was telling me this story matter-of-factly in her home in Athlone with Jimmy beside her not saying a word, just quietly smiling. She suddenly became animated and said:

> Then I received the Eucharist and got a tremendous pain in both heels, which was very unusual. Next the pain disappeared, and so did all other pains in my body. Then followed another Rosary, Benediction, and the final blessing over the sick. It was at this moment I got this magnificent feeling, a wonderful sensation like a whispering breeze telling me I was cured—that if the straps were loosened I could get up and walk. Being very practical, I laughed that off. Anyhow, I knew if I asked anyone to unstrap me, the nurse nearby who had helped me at the Handmaids clinic would put a stop to it. I thought, Jimmy always sorts things out for me. I'll ask him when I get home. Then the nagging thought: But if I'm cured here at Knock and remain passive, maybe the grace will be taken back.
>
> Just then my friend Nuala came over to say hello. I asked her to unstrap me, and I stood up, straight. It was three years since I'd managed that. My arms and hands were back to normal, my head wasn't sagging, and the awful slurring in my speech was gone.

I was taken back to the Handmaids place, and Mrs. Coyne sat me down, and I told her I was cured. Was I seeing clearly? she asked. I said yes, and she handed me a copy of the Knock Annual put out by the Handmaids. The print was clear, and I read the first line on the page: "Why is the Rosary so powerful?" I stopped reading and told her excitedly: "That's our prayer. That's the prayer of our family and our home. It keeps me going during the darkest times."

Marion finished reading the article out loud. It was a special joy to be handed a cup of tea, to be able to hold it steady and drink it without a straw. Judy Coyne's late husband, Judge Liam Coyne, had written a history of Knock with descriptions of shrine miracles, so she questioned Marion carefully for future reference.

Gerry Glynn had left Athlone at 9 A.M., and it was now nearly 6 P.M. He thought he should get Marion home, lest she get exhausted. "I sat up straight the whole way home in the ambulance, not even leaning back", she said. She has a keen sense of fun and decided to surprise Jimmy, asking Gerry to wheel her from the ambulance in her chair. As Gerry wheeled her in, Jimmy asked, "How was Knock?" She replied deadpan, "Ah, it was all right. Sure, why would anybody bother going down there!" Then, as they reached the patio, she got out of the chair and said: "Look, Jimmy, I can walk." "Oh, God, Mar," he gasped, "don't!" Said Marion, "I went over and put my arms around him, and I never saw a man crying like that."

They contacted Dr. Patrick O'Meara by telephone. He feared they were exaggerating, that she was experiencing merely a temporary euphoria resulting from the fervor at the Knock shrine. He came the next day and was bewildered.

Marion's leg muscles should have been wasted and unable to support walking after three years of nonuse, but she was walking. Her catheter had been draining pus and blood because of the kidney he was due to operate on that week. Now it ran clear. "Marion, you were very sick when I saw you on Friday", said the doctor. "Something wonderful has happened. I've never see it happen before. What do we do now?" He finally suggested they play it safe—"Stay in bed while I check you each day." Three days later he agreed she could forget bed and wheelchair. Leave the catheter in, though, he added. Sometimes an operation is needed to remove one that has been in such a long time.

Two weeks later Dr. O'Meara said he was sending the nurse to try to remove the catheter. Marion became apprehensive. Would it be a problem? Was the healing only partial and temporary? "When I don't know what to do, I pray the Rosary, which I did", she said. "The nurse came and removed the catheter, and everything worked normally. I've never had kidney problems since. Nor have I had any pain. Since my Knock experience in 1989, I've never taken as much as an aspirin."

I had read and heard a lot about Marion Carroll before meeting her. With the blessing and urging of her ordinary, Bishop Colin O'Reilly, she has accepted invitations in Ireland and abroad to tell the story of her cure. The bishop and Marion hope through these public meetings to counter the strong antigospel messages in modern society. I kept meeting people who had heard her and were charmed by her freedom from "airs" and pretentiousness. An American magazine put her on its cover and devoted a full page to the cure in November 1994. A television station in Australia did a feature on her. Just before setting out on my world-circling journey to meet miracle cases, I read a large article on her in the Irish *Sunday Tribune* of April 6, 1997. All this prepared me for a wonderful and leisurely interview with Marion and Jimmy in August 1997. Their home and lives have been joyful but frugal. She has gone anywhere she has been asked to speak.

Marion Carroll and husband, Jimmy, August 1997.

Jimmy has gone with her, as silent support, as often as possible. After I had asked her all my questions, she said, "Sure, I get exhausted with all the talking and traveling. But praying before the Blessed Sacrament restores my energy. Prayer is the real answer to all our problems. I feel sad when I come across priests who seem too busy to find time for prayer. I'm sure that's why we've had priests' sex scandals. I met a priest recently who complained of loneliness, suggesting celibacy was the problem. I told him he was wrong, and he'd solve his problem with a deeper prayer life. He didn't like my straight talk!"

As I sat in the train going back to Dublin, I knew why people had told me Marion wins people by her straight talk and refusal to dispense "cheap grace". It reminded me of the tending-to-be-cynical barrister and journalist Patrick Marnham. In his book *Lourdes*, he said among the pilgrims he saw "religion of the people . . . that challenges the dominant Catholicism of the intellect, that subtle, temporizing, qualified faith . . . instead of the robust faith of those Christ came to save".

Marnham has seen too much lying, hypocrisy and media hype not to be cynical of our present society. He discovered a different world at Lourdes—if you will spare him some testy outbursts at the human foibles of some native Lourdais and Lourdes pilgrims! He wrote of "the intense happiness on the faces of the sick" who have discovered at Lourdes that suffering has "meaning and use". The Lourdes Grotto, "once the desolate scene of fantastic visions . . . has become responsible for the health or happiness of thousands of incurably sick and the comfort of millions of their healthy companions". For so many, Lourdes, and similar pilgrim shrines like Knock, have become "a direct experience of divine power . . . and a passionate return to the certainties". Marnham has some good pages on the exacting examinations carried out by the Medical Bureau to establish a miraculous cure. Having quoted Cardinal Newman—"A miracle is no argument to one who is deliberately, and on principle, an atheist"—he mentioned cases of modern doctors who refuse to study Lourdes miracles on principle.

Sixteen-year-old René Scher went on pilgrimage to Lourdes in 1966 from the northeast of France. He had been quite blind since childhood, when an operation went wrong. When Bishop Fox of Wrexham (West England) blessed the sick with the Blessed Sacrament, René Scher's sight was restored. The Medical Bureau confirmed this that same day. However, the doctors at the Metz institute for the blind where René had resided refused the Lourdes Medical Bureau's formal requests for documentation on his case. There have been not a few similar cases where doctors, because of their ideology that miracles cannot happen (faith in reverse?), have refused all cooperation with the Lourdes Medical Bureau in the investigation of an alleged cure.

Collier's Encyclopedia calls Blaise Pascal "one of the greatest minds of the seventeenth century". He left his mark in secular sciences—he pioneered the principles of hydrodynamics and hydrostatics, he invented the syringe and hydraulic press, he perfected the barometer, he made the West's first calculating machine, and he gave Pascal's theorem to mathematics. However, he abandoned all these studies to pursue "absolute truth". He was convinced he experienced it on November 23, 1654, when he wrote on a small page that he was still carrying on his person when he died in 1662: "FIRE. God of Abraham, God of Isaac, God of Jacob. Not of philosophers and scholars. Certainty, certainty, heartfelt joy, peace. God of Jesus Christ." After that he gave himself to prayer, and to writing and discussions devoted to one purpose, to bring others to this faith. He said that to find absolute truth you need to add something vital to your scientific searching. The human mind, no matter how scientific, he pointed out, can be most devious and self-seeking. You need an honest heart to find the deepest truths. He added, "The heart has reasons that reason knows nothing of."

Disappointed with the motives of some with whom he had controversies, he wrote in *Pensées*, "There is enough light for those who desire only to see, and enough darkness for those of a contrary disposition."

Some days after interviewing Marion, I went to Knock. It was a squally day. Gusts of wind drove rain into our faces. That did not stop the pilgrims walking in groups around the original church of the apparitions, heads bowed under umbrellas, reciting the Rosary in subdued voices. Monsignor Grealy met me very warmly, answered my questions and arranged for me to interview two people closely associated with Marion's cure. I have written of the first, Judy Coyne.

The second was Dr. Diarmuid Murray, in charge of the shrine clinic. I asked his opinion of Marion's case. "When she was ill in the seventies and eighties we did not have the new test to identify MS absolutely", he said. "Some doctors have said she did not have it at all—though none of these seem actually to have examined her! To me and to her own Dr. Pat O'Meara, who is a friend from medical school by the way, putting an absolutely correct name to very physical symptoms is not the central point. Doctors have only gradually been able to define and delineate diseases. There is no doubt in my mind, or in Dr. O'Meara's, that Marion Carroll's instantaneous recovery is beyond medical explanation."

There was a recent and famous Australian politician about whom a media commentator said, "If you accused him, for instance, of stealing your property, he would sternly reply, 'But your dog has rabies!' He'd do it with such belligerence that before you knew it, the discussion shifted from your property to your dog and rabies." I see something similar happening in some of the attacks on modern miracles. Words and ideas are thrown out covering all manner of things except the unexplained fact of the instantaneous cure.

Chapter 3

PEADER CLARKE

"Mary, You're Not Listening"

I HAD HEARD ABOUT Peader Clarke's cure while I was still in Sydney. ("Peader" is Gaelic for "Peter" and is pronounced "Padda".) On arriving in Dublin, I had no trouble in tracing him. He is well known from his talks and the video documentary made about his cure. On a beautiful summer's morning in August 1997, I walked through Stephen's Green park to nearby Peader's office, which is just down from the huge Carmelite Fathers' church.

I took an instant liking to him as he greeted me warmly, asked his staff to look after the phones and led me to a quiet back room. Peader is endowed with more than a share of Irish charm and humor. "I enjoy an occasional smoke", he said. "Would you mind?" "Go right ahead", I replied and marveled at his deftness in quickly rolling a cigarette. "I had to give a talk on my cure recently", he went on, "and had a puff at interval. Two old nuns saw me and looked horrified.

But I told them our Lady said nothing to me about an occasional cigarette." He gave a mischievous chuckle.

"When I was nine years old I went down with a bad dose of yellow jaundice", he began. "I remember worried-looking doctors consulting with my mother and putting me into an isolation ward. I was in the hospital for several months, and I suppose that really was the start of my physical problems. As a boy I loved sports—soccer, hurling and other athletics. After my hospitalization I would be running, and suddenly my legs would lose power and topple me. At other times my hands would feel strange, or I'd become dizzy, or my eyes would get out of focus. The doctor simply put it down to vertigo. He didn't seem to worry, so neither did I.

"I was working as a bus conductor when I met Terry Whelan, and it was love at first sight! Like me, the Whelans were Dubliners. We married, and I decided bus conducting would not bring in enough money for us both, so I became a taxi driver. However those 'vertigo' symptoms were now intensifying."

While Peader was driving, his foot would suffer a "spasm" and slip off the brake or clutch pedal. Terry, noticing the deterioration, urged him to get a second opinion about the "vertigo".

I was feeling frustrated and apprehensive, too, and feared what a second opinion might be. Then came the climax. I found it difficult negotiating the Dublin traffic that day, especially at traffic lights. I was finding it hard to judge the distances of cars ahead of me and bumped several, but not hard. I was now feeling peculiar and decided to go home. Arriving there, I could not get out of the car! I could only lean on the horn until Terry came and helped me inside.

I began a series of visits to Dublin's Beaumont Hospital. On the third or fourth visit, I started to get off a waiting-room chair when my name was called, and I just keeled over!

They carried me to a bed and began a series of tests. One day a doctor came into my room and rather tensely began drawing medical diagrams and then awkwardly explaining them. I relieved him of his embarrassment by asking him straight out if I had multiple sclerosis. He said yes and immediately added that he had an appointment and must go! Terry was in shock, but I experienced a strange relief. For her MS was a death sentence. For me it was a name for my miseries.

That was 1988, and I spent the best part of the next year in the hospital, but still I was getting rapidly worse. My speech became slurred and jumbled. I began having bad memory lapses. Terry would come on a visit, and I'd think, "I know that face. I've met her somewhere. Where?" I was soon unable to get out of bed and had become incontinent.

Peader and Terry had now been married eleven years, and one great sorrow was having no children. Medical expenses had eaten away their savings, so Terry, despite wanting to be beside Peader, had to go to work. Her job was serving drinks in the Alsa Sports and Social Club at Dublin Airport. Her fellow workers came to learn of Peader's plight and took up a collection and presented a very surprised Terry with money for two round-trip tickets to Lourdes. But Terry's excitement was chilled when the doctors said the journey to Lourdes was unthinkable. Peader in all probability would never make it back alive. Dr. Sean Murphy of Beaumont Hospital described the patient's debilitated state in the video documentary on Peader's cure.

Terry explained the offer to Peader in one of his lucid moments. He said he had one foot in the grave anyhow, so why not go? Terry's mother, Sheila Whelan, decided she could help, so the three booked into the next Irish pilgrimage. Before leaving they took Peader to say farewell to his mother, hospitalized by a stroke that left her half paralyzed and without speech. Peader remembers how encouraged he was when she held up her worn prayer book in her good hand. "She was simply saying 'God will take care of you'", he said.

As they set out for the airport, the hospital's grim predictions already seemed to be coming true! Peader deteriorated and remembers nothing of the plane trip. He recalled becoming conscious at Lourdes, looking up at the statue of the Crowned Virgin in the giant esplanade. "Gazing at her face," he said, "I lost all my fear of death. Dying was going home to God; a great peace swept over me. 'Ah,' I thought, 'this is my Lourdes miracle.'

"I remember little of the days that followed, except for the last day. We were at Mass at the Grotto, and the priest, probably Father Martin Ryan of our pilgrimage, told us in the homily that 'love is not love until you give it away. Don't pray for yourself; pray for the others.' I began doing that. I saw Terry and her mother were crying, so I asked our Lady to fix up whatever was troubling them!

"Next I remember Nurse Kay Hogan from our pilgrimage pointing to the white stones marking the spot where Saint Bernadette knelt during the apparitions of our Lady in 1858. I thought I'd love to kneel down there and pray, too, and tried to slither off the wheelchair. I ended up on the ground on all fours!"

The nurse and another pilgrim quickly lifted Peader back into his wheelchair, and Nurse Hogan explained in the video how she was suddenly and deeply moved. Looking up at the Virgin's statue, she pleaded, "Our Lady, please think of something. This man is special." When the group began moving away from the Grotto, Peader noticed his wife and Sheila were still crying. He said he complained to Mary, "You are not listening to my prayers. They are still crying."

They wheeled him back to his room on the third floor of the Tara Hotel, cleaned him up and got him into bed. He said,

I was in a lot of pain in my whole body. It seemed to be inside my bones. My stomach was hurting from an ulcer, no doubt caused by all the medication. I had now given up on wanting to live or make it home to Dublin. But I was at peace and knew this was a gift from God. Then I thought, "But what about Terry? It will distress her to see me die. I must get her out of the room, and I'll die alone. Nurse will find me on her rounds and break it gently to Terry." I could not speak but made noises and signs, and Terry and Sheila understood. They drew the blinds, turned off the lights and left for their nearby room.

I closed my eyes and waited for merciful death when one of those spasms hit me, so I ended up on the floor. Another spasm twisted my head, and I found myself looking directly at the crucifix on the wall. I got a fright at first, because I could see it despite there being no light. Then I said as a kind of prayer to him, "Let's give it one more go at staying alive." Suddenly I saw a most beautiful woman standing by the crucifix. I cannot describe the beauty except to call it total sinlessness. That may not make sense to anyone else, but . . . Anyhow, she smiled at me, and I felt sure it was the Mother of Jesus.

Then I thought, no, I was hallucinating from all the drugs the nurse had been giving me. So I rubbed my eyes, but the woman was still there. Now she was with Saint Bernadette, in front of the Lourdes Grotto as it was last century. There were many people there in great physical distress. A conviction swept over me that medicine could no longer help them, only prayer. I must pray for them.

Then our Lady stopped smiling at me, looked at the crucifix and turned back to me again. Her lips did not move, but she seemed to be saying, "Look at my suffering."

I became conscious that I was standing. But hadn't I been thrown from my bed to the floor, and wasn't I unable to stand up by myself? Maybe I was dead? I looked at my bare feet and discovered I could move my toes and my feet! I walked out into the corridor and knocked on the room where my wife was. Sheila opened the door, gasped and asked how I got there. She looked down the corridor for a helper or my wheelchair.

Terry stepped out, and they both became very excited and took me into their room. We all knelt, said a decade of the Rosary, got up and sat on a bed. Terry said I seemed to be glowing, and I could feel energy surging through me and making me feel stronger by the minute. Sheila said: "Peader, the gash is gone." Two days before, while Terry was washing me in my room, I had a violent spasm, and gashed my forehead on a hard object. The nurse said I'd need at least six stitches, but I shook my head meaning no, no stitches. I was in too much pain already. Now, two nights later, I put my hand to my forehead and could feel no hint of a gash.

Back to the video, where Terry took up the story: "I ran to the elevator and went down to the night watchman in the lobby. He was asleep, with his head on his hands. It was now well after midnight. I was so excited that he found it hard to understand me. . . . I asked him urgently to get Nurse Hogan from Hotel Astoria on the phone. He did, and I said, 'Nurse, Peader needs you. Can you come immediately?' She woke her brother-in-law Tommy, and he accompanied her."

Sheila Whelan took over from her daughter on the video: "When Terry left for the lobby, I asked Peader to go out into the corridor to see if he could walk any distance. 'Walk?' he answered. 'I'm going to run.' And he proceeded to do that, up and down. When Terry stepped out of the elevator, I called, 'Look what he can do!' With that, he ran down the corridor, picked her up and twirled her in the air."

Nurse Hogan appeared next on the video and said with great excitement, "He ran down to the elevator door and nearly squeezed me to death. Then he sat Tommy and me down in the room and told us the whole story. I could hardly believe what I was seeing and hearing. Finally Peader said, 'Right, let's all go down and have a drink!' "

Peader Clarke with the Tara Hotel crucifix, 1997.

They went down, and Terry decided to take the camera
and snap some photos "to prove it wasn't all a dream. I kept
fearing I'd wake up from this beautiful dream. Maybe the
others felt the same. No one wanted to go back to bed!
When we hit the streets the next morning, the news spread
quickly." The video carries the photos they took that momentous night, May 7, 1989.

Peader reported to the Medical Bureau and presented the

medical certificate written by his doctor, Dr. Sean Murphy. The bureau doctors studied it, examined Peader and told him to return for another examination in twelve months' time.

They returned to Dublin and went straight to Peader's hospitalized mother. She smiled as if it was all very natural and held her battered prayer book aloft. He went to visit her often and used to read her prayers from the old book. She died that year on July 20. "I saw she was dying and was able to let her go peacefully to the Lord", Peader said.

My first interview with Peader took several hours. After it he showed me a photo of his wife and said, "You can see she is very beautiful. She has tons of personality and energy. It would surely have been the easier thing to slip away quietly when the hospital gave no hope of me recovering! But Terry didn't! She kept her marriage vows. All through the crises she was rock solid. I never heard a single complaint or saw a tear or sign of bitterness or frustration. After my cure my mother-in-law told me Terry used to go to her and sob her heart out!" Since the cure they have had their longed-for children—Mary Bernadette and then Luke.

Peader continued:

When you read about Lourdes cures, you sometimes come across the expression "our Lady's souvenir", meaning scars or marks left in the cured person. With me our Lady's souvenir was far more serious, some arthritis in the knees and hip— thanks be to God. I add that because I believe some pain helps me remember the mission I think our Lady has given me. It is to pray for and help people who are suffering. If I were totally healed, I think it might be easy for me to forget our Lady's request. The hotel gave me that crucifix I told you of. I take it with me when I pray with people who are suffering or sick.

Terry's workmates paid our fare to Lourdes when we were out of money. We decided to do the same and take others in need to Lourdes. We formed a committee to raise funds. The first year we took ten people. This year (1997) we took 145. One of them was a young mother from the United Kingdom dying of cancer. She was not a Catholic—her sister living in Limerick asked for our help. When she arrived at Lourdes, she was only interested in herself and her own sickness. She was angry and bitter. I spent about ninety minutes each day talking with her about the message of Lourdes, and gradually she changed. She began to notice sick people worse than herself and to feel their pain. She started joining us in prayer and found real faith in God. She returned to London at peace with God and herself, and that is how she died, according to her sister.

Dr. Roger Pilon, who until 1996 was the doctor permanently on duty at the Medical Bureau, wrote in the July 1996 issue of *Lourdes Magazine* (a fifty-page magazine that comes out ten times a year in five languages): "Every year about 15 miracle cases are presented to the Medical Bureau. Increasingly their healing becomes a conversion, a sign for commitment to the service of others . . . Their devotion to Our Lady and attention to others reveals their conviction of a call, a call to testify to the tenderness of God. . . . As for the unhealed, the vast majority want to return on pilgrimage and relive their painful journey. . . . [They have experienced] the serenity and trust of knowing they are loved by the Father and by their brothers and sisters in the Faith."

While at Lourdes in the early summer of 1997 I met a volunteer nurse, Mary Denahy, from Coolstown, Ireland. When she was a teenager she was taken to Lourdes by her mother. She grew up and married a farmer from County Armagh, and they were blessed with a daughter—a mixed blessing! The little baby had kidney problems, and half a kidney had to be cut out! When the child was two years old, the doctors discovered the good kidney had so deteriorated

*Peader Clarke and his wife, Terry, at Lourdes
several years after the cure.*

that it had to be removed promptly. "Wait until I've taken her
to Lourdes", the mother replied. Mary took her very ill child
to Lourdes immediately and prayed with faith on the knee-
worn pavement before the Grotto. She returned home and
took the child back to the doctors, who discovered the
kidney was perfect. That was twenty years ago, and the child
has grown up in robust health. Mary has gone to help with
the sick at Lourdes every year since then, sometimes twice a
year. "I've never seen anyone rise from a wheelchair," she
added, "but two of my friends, who also go as volunteer
nurses, have. The greatest miracles I've seen are mothers
coming with children who are very sick, crippled, deformed
or retarded. The mothers can look so distressed when they
arrive. They go home peaceful and joyful, now understanding that nursing their disadvantaged little ones is a special
vocation, given them personally by God."

The day after I met Mary Denahy, a French journalist, Christine Bray, loaned me a recently published book—*Expect a Miracle*, by a well-published American author, Dan Wakefield.[1] This Protestant writer gave considerable space to the phenomenon of serenity and joy he observed in Lourdes, a city that is host to more than seventy thousand sick pilgrims annually. He wrote of meeting one very disgruntled Irish lass, of college age, who had come to Lourdes only to get her parents off her back! She angrily told the author that the crass commercialism of the souvenir shops and the whole atmosphere of the place turned her off completely. She could not wait till the pilgrimage was over and she could get clear of the depressing place. Wakefield asked her to do him a favor—to drop him a line if her opinion changed by the end of her stay. She later did write when back in Dublin, and he quoted her reply in his book. She found her cynicism gradually changing as she helped care for the sick pilgrims each day. She would accompany them to the baths and to the afternoon procession, when the sick are celebrated as very important persons. Then they receive everyone's prayers and often tears, and the bishop's blessing. She became fascinated by the procession each night, when a huge crowd sang to the Virgin and carried candles in white cardboard holders. At the chorus of the Lourdes hymn, the "Ave, Ave, Ave Maria", they would raise their candles on high, "as if they were offering a toast to our Lady", wrote the young woman. "Before coming to Lourdes, I used to go to Sunday Mass with my head down, in case university classmates saw me. Now I'm back in Dublin and go to Mass with my head held high!"

There is no doubt in my mind, or in his, or in his friends', that Peader Clarke was healed miraculously. However, a doctor who knows the case and accepts it as a miracle told me the

[1] Dan Wakefield, *Expect a Miracle: The Miraculous Things That Happen to Ordinary People* (New York: HarperCollins, 1995).

Lourdes Medical Bureau will almost certainly never accept it because of the residual arthritis in his knees and hip. Hence it fails one of the seven conditions laid down in 1734 by Pope Benedict XIV for acceptance of a cure as miraculous. The conditions are:

1. The malady must be grave and impossible or very difficult to cure.
2. The malady was not in a state of decline.
3. There was no use of a possibly effective medicament.
4. The cure was instantaneous.
5. The cure was complete (a perfect cure of the malady).
6. There was not beforehand any noteworthy decrease of symptoms or a "crisis" that might provide a natural explanation.
7. The cure was permanent.

As you will quickly discover if you research the Lourdes Medical Bureau, the doctors there refuse to examine the cure of any sickness that could possibly be psychological in cause. Only cases of illnesses that were organic—and proven by X rays, biopsies and such medical tests—are ever considered by the bureau. This is not to say psychoses or neuroses are not cured at Lourdes. However, the Medical Bureau confines itself only to observable and medically proven organic illnesses, healed quite completely.

Chapter 4

JOHN TRAYNOR

Gallipoli, Liverpool and Lourdes

JOHN TRAYNOR was born in 1883 in Liverpool. His mother was Irish, and her self-confidence and faith had been forged in the terrible fires of the Irish famine, evictions and migrations that saw the population go from eight million to five million in the second half of the nineteenth century. She handed on that confidence and faith to her son so well that, though she died while he was still a boy, it never wavered all his life. He went to Saint Patrick's Primary School in Liverpool until he was twelve, when with family resources in short supply, he left to join the "school of hard knocks" at sea. By the age of sixteen John (Jack) could say he had traveled "one thousand miles up the Amazon River". By the age of thirty he had crossed all the major sea routes. He was tough physically and spiritually. "My first duty in a foreign port was to find a Catholic church and fetch as many shipmates as possible to Sunday Mass", he said.

In 1907 Jack became a stoker in the Royal Navy Reserve. On the day World War I broke out, August 4, 1914, he was in it. Trained for one month at Dorset, he was sent to Dunkirk. The Belgians had denied the German government's request of free passage for the German Army attacking France. The Germans invaded Belgium and would soon occupy most of the country. The small Belgian Army resisted, and Jack's battalion was sent in support. It was to little avail. The German juggernaut smashed the defense lines. One of Jack's commanding officers, a man named Dukinfield, was badly wounded, and Jack carried him for miles on his powerful shoulders. Just near Bruges a German shell burst close by, and shrapnel hit Jack in the head. That was October 8, 1914. He was carried away unconscious and was operated on, and he regained consciousness only five weeks later in a hospital in Deal, England. The doctors finally discharged him, and he rejoined his unit. Immediately promoted to petty officer first class, he was sent to Egypt. In a firefight with Turks east of the Suez Canal, he was hit in the right knee by a bullet. "It was a clean wound, and I was soon on my feet and in uniform again, on the S.S. *River Clyde*, heading for Gallipoli", he said. He landed with the first boats at dawn on April 25, 1915, as a captain of machine guns. The Turks had been waiting, and Allied casualties were very high. On May 8 in a wild bayonet charge at Turk trenches, Jack ran into an arc of machine-gun bullets. Two passed through the right side of his chest without doing much damage. The third bullet traveled up the inside of his right arm, lodging under the right collarbone. It severed the brachial plexus and the large nerves in the axilla. English doctor Francis Izard, X.R.C.S. England, L.R.C.P., London, who studied and wrote about the Traynor case, said: "The nerves which were severed supply sensation to the skin of the arm and motivate the muscles. Traynor's right arm as a result suffered loss of sensation, paralysis and, subsequently, atrophy." Evacuated to Alexandria, Traynor was first operated on by Sir Frederick Treves, who unsuccessfully attempted to suture the severed nerves. On the voyage back to England in the S.S. *Gurka*, a similar operation was attempted by a Major Ross, with no success. During this voyage in August 1915, the first attack of epilepsy occurred, nearly ten months after the head injury during the retreat from Antwerp in Belgium.

At Haslar Hospital another unsuccessful attempt was made to suture the nerves on September 2. In November the naval surgeon told Jack his arm would always be useless and it would be better to amputate it. Jack refused. On August 5, 1916, the Medical Pension Board gave him an 80 percent pension.

He was discharged from military service and placed under the care of Drs. Warrington and Nelson, who asked Dr. McMurray to attempt another suture of the divided nerves. This operation took place on November 27, 1916, and for the fourth time was unsuccessful. The epileptic attacks began to become more and more frequent, becoming the dominant factor in the situation. In September 1917 Jack's pension was augmented to 100 percent. Ten months of 1918 were spent in a special institution for epileptics, Mandall House, in Bromborough, Cheshire. From here he was sent to Northern Hospital in Alder, Liverpool, where his wife and children lived. In 1919 it was decided to try electric treatment and reeducation of the muscles on the right arm at Alder Hey Hospital. The treatment did no good, and epileptic attacks increased in severity.

He was transferred to Springfields Hospital under the Ministry of Pensions. Here in April 1920 Major Montserrat, evidently believing the epilepsy was traumatic in origin and the result of the first head injury, trephined the skull in the right parietal region (leaving a circular opening slightly under an inch in diameter). This procedure also was unsuccessful. The epileptic attacks continued; sometimes he had three a day.

An ambulance took him home to his distraught wife and children at 121 Grafton Street, Liverpool. He could neither walk nor stand. "Both legs were partially paralyzed," noted Dr. Izard, "and there was loss of control over the bladder and rectum. A state of unconsciousness often followed his numerous epileptic fits. The right arm was atrophied. On the skull was an opening which showed the pulsations of the brain. On coughing there was a protrusion of dura matter, the membrane covering the brain. There was much headache and loss of memory."

Britain's losses in World War I were huge, and all the government could afford as full pension was about three dollars a week. Jack's wife had to do everything for him and so from August 1922 on received a small "constant attention allowance". The Ministry of Pensions gave him a wheelchair and an air cushion to help the bedsores at the base of his spine. Jack Traynor stated, "All feeling and power of my limbs left me altogether. At that stage (early July 1923) I had not moved my right arm in eight years."

A letter came from the Pensions Ministry stating that he could move into the Hospital for Incurables, Mossley Hill, on July 14. That was a shock for Jack. Definitely incurable! But a chance visit by Mrs. Cunningham dramatically changed his gloom to hope. The parish priest, she said, was taking one pound as down payment for a place in the Lancashire Lourdes pilgrimage. The total cost was thirteen pounds. The group would travel to Lourdes by boat and train, leaving July 21.

Jack called out for his wife and told her to bring the sovereign (worth one pound) his brother had given him. He was keeping it in a box "for some special emergency". His wife protested at first against the trip to Lourdes, but she finally got the sovereign and gave it to Mrs. Cunningham to give the parish priest. In no time the latter was down at the home asking Jack to change his mind about going. When the patient persisted, the priest said, "Jack, you'll die on the way and bring grief to everyone", only to be told, "I've paid my deposit. I'm going!" Two doctors treating Jack and then the Pensions Ministry heard of his proposed pilgrimage, and all protested adamantly. "Every one of them said it would be suicide", Jack later wrote, adding, "The priest came again and flung himself across my bed, begging me to give up the idea." Everyone except his wife and two relatives was now against the trip. "To raise the £12, the balance due on my ticket, we sold some of our belongings, and my wife even pawned some of her bits of jewellery", he wrote.

Newspapers love a controversy, all the more so if there is a church fight, and several articles on the proposed trip of the paralyzed ex-soldier appeared in the Liverpool media. Jack was not happy with all the attention he was getting. He had his brother Francis push his wheelchair to the railway station via side streets. At the station many in the large crowd—four hundred Liverpool pilgrims and many to see them off—crowded around the now newspaper-famous Traynor. So many impeded the wheelchair's progress that he missed the first train! The priest again begged Jack to stay at home, suggesting the missed train was a sign from God. "There's a second train," replied Jack, "and I'll be on it, in the coal tender if necessary!" "You'll die on the way", said the cleric. Jack retorted, "Then I'll die in a good cause!"

It was a rough trip, much worse than Traynor had imagined, and he arrived in Lourdes the next day, July 22, 1923, very physically distressed. He looked so bad that one of his fellow pilgrims wrote to his wife warning her she would not see him return alive! "I was in a terrible condition, as my wounds and sores had not been freshly bandaged since I left

Jack Traynor the invalid leaving for Lourdes, July 21, 1923,
Lime Street Station, Liverpool.

Liverpool", Jack wrote. A Protestant nurse from Liverpool and her sister were in Lourdes, heard of the arrival of the Lancashire pilgrims and went to see them. They recognized Traynor and volunteered to nurse him. He was in the Asile Hospital, which cared for sick pilgrims who had no money.

Jack looked very bad but insisted on being taken to the *piscines*, baths filled with water from the spring that appeared when Bernadette scooped out mud where "the Lady" had pointed on February 25, 1858. While on the second trip to the *piscines*, a severe epileptic fit shook Traynor violently. "I felt something burst in my chest, and blood flowed freely from my mouth. The doctors were very alarmed and when I came round—very quickly—refused to let me go to the baths, saying I would surely collapse. I insisted, putting the brake on my wheeled car with my usable left hand, refusing to change my mind. The doctors gave in. . . . When I was taken out of the water some change unknown to me had taken place. It marked the end of my epileptic fits. . . . However, my pain, paralysis and sleeplessness continued until my ninth and last immersion in the *piscines*. My legs became violently agitated, so much so that I almost emptied the bath. The *brancardiers* [stretcher bearers] and attendants were terribly alarmed, thinking I was in a fit. They held me down. I struggled to get on my feet, feeling that I could easily do so, and wondered why everybody seemed to be against me. When I was taken out of the bath, I cried from sheer weakness and exhaustion." *Brancardiers* threw Jack's clothes back on him and rushed round to the huge square in front of the Rosary Church for the procession and the blessing of the sick with the Eucharist.

The archbishop of Rheims came along the lines of the sick in their wheelchairs and stretchers, carrying the Blessed Sacrament in a gold monstrance. He raised it above Jack in the sign of the cross and moved on. Jack continued his narrative: "He had just passed by when I realized that a great change had taken place in me. My right arm, which had been dead since 1915, was violently agitated. I burst the bandages and blessed myself—for the first time in years. I attempted to rise from my stretcher, but the *brancardiers* had been watching me. I suppose I had a bad name for my obstinacy. They held me down, and a doctor or a nurse gave me a hypo [a shot with a hypodermic needle]. Apparently they thought I was hysterical and about to create a scene. They rushed me back to the Asile Hospital."

Jack was very well known to the doctors and volunteer nursing staff. There were the argument with the priest and the newspaper publicity before he left Liverpool. He was so ill on the train journey that a number of them wanted to unload him if they stopped at a station with a hospital. The fits distressed everyone and convinced many—including the woman who wrote the warning letter to his wife—that he would die on their hands. Then there were his violent hemorrhage from the mouth before entering the baths, his stubborn locking of the wheelchair and his almost emptying the bath with the violence of his thrashing legs! Jack now had quite a reputation! The doctors feared he would have more fits.

He continued: "They had me in a small ward on the ground floor. As I was such a troublesome case, they stationed *brancardiers* in relays to watch me and keep me from doing anything foolish. . . . The effect of the hypos began to wear off during the night. . . . I was awake for most of the night. Early in the morning I heard the chimes in the Basilica playing the air of the Lourdes 'Ave Maria'. I jumped out of bed. First I knelt on the floor to finish the Rosary I had been saying. Then I dashed for the door, pushed aside the two *brancardiers* and ran out. . . . I may say here I had not walked since 1919, and my weight was down to eight stone [112 pounds]." (When Jack wrote this account several years later, he was almost double this weight.)

"Out in the open now I ran toward the Grotto"—where our Lady had appeared to Saint Bernadette—"which is about two hundred yards from the Asile Hospital. The stretch of ground was graveled then, and I was barefoot. I ran all the way without getting the least mark or cut on my bare feet.

The *brancardiers* were running after me, but they could not catch up. When they reached the Grotto, there I was on my knees, still in my night clothes, praying to our Lady and thanking her . . . for about twenty minutes. . . . At the far end of the Rosary Square stands the statue of Our Lady Crowned. My mother had always taught me that when you ask a favor of our Lady or wish to show her some special veneration, you should make a sacrifice. I had no money to offer, as I had spent my last few shillings on rosaries and medals for my wife and children. Kneeling there before our Lady, I made the only sacrifice I could think of. I resolved to give up cigarettes."

As often happens with Lourdes cures, the magnitude of what had occurred had not yet sunk in. Jack returned to the hospital and wondered why, when he went into the washroom and greeted the other men with a cheery "good morning", "none of them answered back—they just looked at me in a scared way. I wondered why. . . . Later a Mr. Cunningham came to talk to me. I could see that he found it hard to contain his excitement. . . . He said: 'Good morning, Jack. Are you feeling all right?' 'Yes', I answered. 'Are you feeling all right?' Then I asked, 'What are these people doing outside?' He replied, 'They're there, Jack, because they're glad to see you.' 'Well, it's very nice of them, and I'm glad to see them, but I wish they'd leave me alone.' He told me that the priest who had opposed my coming was anxious to speak to me. He was in a hotel in the town, and the problem was how to get through the crowd."

When Jack Traynor stepped outside, the crowd surged around him and Cunningham. It took some appeals before they moved back and let the two set out for the understandably chagrined and chastened priest. (Jack kindly left his name out of the account.)

"The priest too asked me if I was all right. I was quite

surprised by the question. I told him I felt quite well, thanks, and that I hoped he did, too. He broke down and began to cry. . . . That day was a nightmare of excitement and crowds. I was the center of attraction for all the people in Lourdes, it seemed to me." Someone had found Jack some footwear. "I put on a pair of shoes for the first time in four and a half years." It was July 26.

Before the train left with the Lancashire pilgrims the next morning, Jack was examined at the famous Lourdes Medical Bureau by three doctors who had come with the Lancashire pilgrims, Drs. Finn, Marley and Azurdia. The same three had examined Jack, whom many thought was dying, on July 24, two days after the pilgrimage arrived. The Medical Bureau asks doctors to leave signed reports, and you can still see the July 24 original stating that

> John Traynor of 121 Grafton St., Liverpool, is suffering from the following conditions:
>
> (1) Epileptic (We ourselves saw several attacks during his journey to Lourdes).
>
> (2) Paralysis involving the median, musculo-spinal and ulnar nerves of the right arm, the hand is "en griffe" (clawlike), deformity and wasting of all the muscles of the right upper limb, wasting of the right pectoral and axillary muscles, wrist drop and muscular atrophy.
>
> (3) The trephine opening in the right parietal region is about 2.5 c.m. The pulsations of the brain are visible. A metal plate covers the trephine orifice.
>
> (4) There is absence of voluntary movement of the legs, with loss of sensibility.
>
> (5) Incontinence of urine and faeces.
>
> [Signed by] Drs. Finn, Marley and Azurdia.

Now, on July 27, the same three doctors signed a statement, still preserved at the Medical Bureau, as follows:

> (1) He can walk perfectly.

(2) He has recovered the use and function of his right arm.

(3) He has recovered sensation in his legs.

(4) The opening in his skull has diminished considerably.

On Friday, July 27, Jack boarded the train for home, still in something of a strange state of unreality. The full impact of his cure had not yet sunk in. He wrote: "I was still in a sort of a daze. At one of the stops the door of my compartment opened, and to my amazement I saw the red skull cap of Archbishop Keating. . . . I knelt to get his blessing. He raised me up saying, 'John, I think I should be getting your blessing.' I could not understand why he said that. Then he led me over, and we both sat down on the bed." (Despite his protests, Jack had been put in a first-class compartment.)

> Looking at me, he said, "John, do you realize how ill you have been and that you have been miraculously cured by the Blessed Virgin?" Then everything came back to me, the memory of my years of illness and the sufferings of the journey to Lourdes and how ill I had been at Lourdes itself. I began to cry, and the archbishop began to cry, and we both sat there crying like two children. After a little talk with him I felt composed. Now I realized fully what had happened.
>
> Meanwhile the news of the miracle had been telegraphed to the Liverpool papers. . . . Somebody on the train—Father Quinlan or Father McKinley—said to me I should send my wife a wire. I did not care to make a fuss in a telegram, so I just sent her this message: "Am better—Jack." One of the priests in our parish, Father Dawber, had seen the news in the papers and rushed down to her for fear the shock might be too great. . . . He asked if she had any news of me. She answered: "I had a letter from a woman on the pilgrimage, and it upset me very much. It said Jack was dying and would never leave Lourdes alive. But just today I had a telegram from himself saying he is feeling much better." "But suppose you find Jack improved quite a bit, Mrs. Traynor. Will you promise me you won't get upset?" "To be sure, Father. And

I'll be glad if I see him improved." "Suppose you see him walking, Mrs. Traynor?" "Father, I'm afraid I'll never see Jack walk. But anyhow you can rely on me."

My wife went down to the Lime Street Station with Mrs. Reitdyk. It seemed as if all Liverpool had gathered there. The people had seen the news of the miracle in the evening papers. . . . There were extra police on duty to handle the crowd, while railway officials stood at the entrance to the platform to keep the people from rushing the train. With difficulty my wife and her friend reached the platform gate, where she told the official she was Mrs. Traynor and asked to be allowed through. The man replied: "Well, all I can say is Mr. Traynor must be a Mohammedan, because there are seventy or eighty Mrs. Traynors on the platform already!"

Meanwhile, the railway company had decided that the only safe thing to do was to stop the train outside the station. The archbishop walked toward the crowd, now a huge one . . . and asked the people to be orderly and to promise if they just saw Mr. Traynor walk down the platform they would be satisfied and disperse. They answered him they would.

But when I did appear on the platform there was a stampede. The police had to draw their batons to force a passage for my wife and myself to the taxi. My brother got a blow on the side of the head before he could fight his way into the taxi with me. We drove home, and I cannot describe the joy of my wife and children.

The Liverpool *Post and Mercury* carried the news on Monday, July 30, 1923. The heading was "Lourdes Pilgrims Return: Paralysed Man Able to Walk." The article began, "Extraordinary scenes were witnessed at Lime Street Station on Saturday night."

Jack Traynor added an epilogue to his testimony: "I am in the coal and haulage business now. I have four lorries or trucks and about a dozen men working for me. I lift sacks of coal weighing around two hundred pounds with the best of them, and I can do any other work that an able-bodied man can do. But officially I am still classified as 100 percent disabled and permanently incapacitated."

The War Pensions Ministry was given a full report of the restoration of Jack's health. The ministry did not reply, and his full pension kept coming. Later, Dr. Francis Izard, who had thoroughly investigated the case, contacted the pensions office and asked to see its medical notes on the case, pointing out that Traynor himself gave permission. The office refused, giving no reason, and one can almost sympathize with that decision! What a cat among the pigeons a medically proven miracle cure would be! So the pensions doctors just ignored it.

Jack, a man of strong loyalties, asked one of his old teachers from Saint Patrick's Primary to help him with his spelling and grammar when he wrote his official report. Schoolmaster John Murray acquiesced and witnessed Traynor's signature with his own.

Fiercely independent, Jack later wrote: "I never accepted a penny from anybody at the time of my cure or after it. I came back from Lourdes penniless, except for my war pension. I have never permitted any money to come to my family in connection with my cure or the publicity that followed it. Nevertheless . . . I am now comfortably situated, thanks be to God, and my children are well provided for. Three of them have been born since my cure, one a girl, whom I have named Bernadette.

"A large number of conversions in Liverpool have resulted from the miracle. I go now to Lourdes every year and work as a *brancardier*. I have gone twice and three times in one season." *Brancardiers*, of course, are volunteers who pay all their own expenses for the privilege of helping sick pilgrims to Lourdes.

People who claim cures at Lourdes are asked to present themselves within twenty-four hours to the Medical Bureau

ABOVE: *Jack Traynor arriving at Liverpool Station after his cure.*

RIGHT: *Jack Traynor as volunteer* brancardier *at Lourdes, after his cure.*

for a medical examination. They must return the next year for another examination and bring a report from the doctor who treated them before the reported cure. Jack came to the Medical Bureau the following July with this report: "John Traynor, aged 41, living at 121 Grafton St., suffering from gunshot wounds in the head, the chest and from epilepsy, has been under my care since his discharge from [Springfields] Hospital. There have been no epileptic fits. [Signed] Dr. McConnell." The Lourdes Bureau examined him, found him physically healed of all his complaints and told him to report back the following year. The bureau always waits at least several years, and usually more, before making any definitive statement—just in case. There could be fraud, a mistaken diagnosis or temporary improvement due to euphoria. Finally, on July 7, 1926, three full years after Traynor's dramatic "resurrection", as one researcher called it, they were ready. The report was signed by the bureau president, Dr. Vallet, and by the three who were on the original pilgrimage (Drs. Finn, Marley and Azurdia, who signed the before and after statements in July 1923); it was witnessed by Drs. Harrington (of Preston, Lancashire) and Moorkens (of Antwerp, Belgium). It reads: "The right hand is slightly 'en griffe' and shows a little wasting of the interossial muscles. The right forearm is less than the left by one and a half centimeters in circumference. No atrophy of the pectoral or shoulder muscles now exists. The trephine opening has been obliterated; with the finger a slight depression only is found in the bone. There have been no epileptic seizures since the cure in 1923." Dr. Vallet commented that this now vigorously well man was a "pathological museum" when he first arrived at Lourdes. On October 2, 1926, the Lourdes Medical Bureau stated that "this extraordinary cure is beyond and above natural causes".

What of the right hand "slightly en griffe" and the little wasting of the interossial muscles and the "slight depression" where the nearly one-inch hole had been? If God healed Traynor, why these? Dr. Michael Lasalle of the Lourdes Medical Bureau told me in June 1997 that they have medical records of twenty-five hundred cures that are medically inexplicable. However, almost all of the ones I have studied have some small remnant of the sickness left. Lourdes writers call it our Lady's "souvenir" of the cure. It serves a good purpose— reminding miracle recipients of the grace they have received.

Lourdes cure cases, of course, like the people Jesus healed, are not permanently well. They eventually die! John Traynor died on December 7, 1943, when in Catholic churches the liturgical prayers had begun for the next day's feast of the Immaculate Conception. (In 1858, after Bernadette had on three occasions begged "the Lady" to tell her name, Mary used the extraordinary expression "I am the Immaculate Conception.") Traynor's death was in no way connected with

his former illnesses. He died of a strangulated hernia. My
supposition is that the ever-generous, ever-confident boss of
a haulage business did not take younger men's advice about
sixty-year-olds lifting two-hundred-pound bags of coal and
therefore developed that hernia!

A postscript: John Traynor's is not among the canonical
miracles. The Lourdes Medical Bureau passed his cure and
sent the papers to the Liverpool diocesan office. The papers
are missing—the diocesan office says they never arrived. Did
they go astray in the mail or in the diocesan office? No one
knows. However, not a few bishops, knowing there are so
many authenticated miracles and also the costs in time and
money in a canonical inquiry, are not too eager to get
involved in one.[1]

---

[1] Several books tell Jack Traynor's story. They include: *I Met a Miracle*, a
sixteen-page 1965 London Catholic Truth Society pamphlet on the man by
Patrick O'Connor, a famous Columban priest and journalist; Dom Francis
Izard, *The Meaning of Lourdes* (London: Sands and Co., 1938); Ruth Cranston,
The Miracle of Lourdes (New York: Doubleday Image, 1955; reprinted 1988
[Cranston was a Protestant and daughter of a Methodist bishop; her revised
book containing Traynor's story is a classic]); Monsignor Joseph Derry, *Our
Lady of Lourdes* (Dublin: Browne and Nolan, 1957); Don Sharkey, *After Ber-
nadette* (Milwaukee: Bruce Publishing Co., 1945).

Chapter 5

BROTHER LEO

The Accident-Prone Swiss

WHILE IN LOURDES in June 1997, I kept hearing about an Irish nun, Sister Mary Patrick, who had spent forty-nine years working in Lourdes. She nurses the sick, but because she speaks French almost as fluently as English, she is in much demand when translation problems arise. In the course of my conversation with her, interrupted every so often by staff needing her advice, she spoke of miracle cures she had known. With a lovely smile she said, "I'll never forget poor Brother Leo Schwager when he arrived in April 1952. He was bedridden, paralyzed and hardly seemed conscious. I tried to give him some liquid nourishment, and half of it dribbled out of his mouth and down his beard."

Leo Schwager, the seventh of eight children, was born on May 19, 1924. Hardship dogged his youth. He was still in primary school when the Depression hit. His father worked in an embroidery business in nearby Saint Gall—the north-eastern Swiss city that traces its origins to the arrival of the

Irish monk Gall in 614. The embroidery business fell on hard times, and so did the ten members of the Schwager family. About two years later, when Leo was ten, his mother died. When Leo was in his first year of high school, he had a very bad fall from his bicycle, with serious consequences. He began to have memory lapses and found normal concentration on schoolwork extraordinarily difficult. His doctor ordered a period of rest, and after that, as he was still affected by the accident, suggested he leave his normal high school and attend an agricultural school in nearby Flauvil. He found it easier to handle ploughing and milking than schoolbooks. However, due to a lapse in concentration or sheer bad luck, Leo was thrown from a horse in 1945 and was picked up unconscious, suffering serious brain injuries and a broken jaw. Then—and his family could not believe his run of trouble— he contracted diphtheria! He was doing far worse in pacifist Switzerland than many other European youth on World War II battlefields!

He got back on his feet and, at age twenty-one, decided to try out what he had been considering for some time, a vocation as a missionary. His insufficient academic schooling disqualified him from becoming a priest. However, he was happy to be a manual worker and applied successfully to join the Benedictine Missionaries in Fribourg as a brother novice. He worked very happily in the kitchen, but his health became a problem. At the end of 1946 he was troubled with spasmodic double vision. Then late in 1947 a slurring began to affect his speech. "It was as if my tongue was being pressed down with a spoon, and my confreres were unable to understand me easily", he wrote. The doctor told him that probably the fall from the horse and his bout with diphtheria were the root causes, but he could not come up with any medical alleviation.

Leo's Benedictine superiors were impressed with his dedi-

cation and prayer life. Despite the risk of his becoming a
community burden, they called him to first vows at the end
of 1947, on December 8, feast of the Immaculate Conception. Brother Leo was overjoyed by their trust and faced the
future enthusiastically and confidently. But, alas, not for long!
Suddenly he found himself completely paralyzed on the left
side. Doggedly he did all the doctors suggested and sometimes seemed to be improving. Then his health would plummet again, and a little further each time. Of course he
worried that his Benedictine superiors would consider his
now-chronic ill health—which meant he was unable to do
any work at all—a clear indication he had no vocation!

His superior, Dom Notker Mannhart, did not judge men
by visible usefulness. He encouraged the sick monk to "just
trust in God". When Leo's temporary vows ran out, on
December 8, 1950, Dom Mannhart decided that Leo could
take solemn vows, making him a Benedictine for life. Brother
Leo did this joyfully. This great boost to his morale, however,
was matched by no improvement in health. In 1951 he was
hospitalized in Zurich for tests. Chief Doctor Ott gave the
grim news to the monastery—multiple sclerosis at an advanced stage. Since MS is often a difficult disease to diagnose
with certainty, Ott had the patient transferred to the Clinic of
Neurosurgery in Zurich. Dr. Kreienbuhl's extensive tests
confirmed the first diagnosis.

Dom Mannhart had him brought back to the monastery.
Brother Leo later wrote: "My state worsened visibly. All my
organs were suffering. . . . We tried Dr. Evers' diet without
any relief coming. My daily food consisted of wheat germ,
fruit juice, a little honey and sometimes a raw egg. It became
necessary to have a urinary catheter permanently. I weighed
no more than 47 kilograms (103 pounds) for a height of 175
centimeters (5 feet, 9 inches). I had become totally infirm and
was nursed like a small child. Most of the time I could not

manage a single word. Not to be able to speak is one of the worst possible things. . . . The doctor estimated I would not live till summer if my illness continued to worsen at this rate.

"In March 1952, my superior came to my bedroom one morning and said: 'Brother Leo, I had an idea last night. I'm going to send you to Lourdes.' We discussed this, and he said, 'Only the good Lord through the intercession of the Blessed Virgin can help you!'"

Then, disappointment. The registration period of the German-Swiss pilgrimage had passed! The superior appealed to Pilgrimage Director Father Bushel, telling him of the doctor's grim prognosis. "Right, we'll take the poor devil!" was the director's response.

On April 28, 1952, a very feeble Leo was lifted onto the pilgrimage train at Fribourg for the twenty-four-hour journey to Lourdes. Irish Sister Mary Patrick remembered how sorry she felt as she tried to spoon some liquid nourishment into the mouth of the semi-conscious Swiss—only twenty-eight years old but looking like the dying inmate of an old folks' home.

Brother Leo continued the story:

On April 30 we had our first celebration at the Grotto in the morning. For me it was indescribable happiness to find myself in the place where the Blessed Virgin appeared eighteen times to Bernadette.

After Mass I was taken into the baths but felt no relief from my pain. . . . [After lunch] all of us sick were taken again to the Grotto, where we recited the Rosary and listened to a homily. . . . We were asked individually if we'd been to the baths that morning. As I was unable to speak, I was put into the group of sick that had not gone. At a little before 4 P.M. I was plunged again into the water from the spring. No improvement! I even experienced vivid pains and a great uneasiness. I kept making signs to the man pushing my wheelchair to get me back to bed, but the good man did not notice it and took me to the Rosary Esplanade. The other ill were already there waiting for the Blessing of the Sick. . . .

I thought, "Oh well, you can stand a bit more of this in the name of the Lord!" But I was in such a miserable state that I could not even join in the invocations. I was simply there. Next the bishop gave the Blessing of the Sick right in front of me. It was as if an electric shock went over my whole body, from head to foot! I thought, "Good, now I can die in peace." I think I lost consciousness, and everything became blurred.

Then all of a sudden I found myself on my knees in front of the bishop carrying the Blessed Sacrament! I felt wholly well, as if reborn, and all my pain had vanished. Dr. Jeger from Chur, a member of the Swiss pilgrimage, immediately rushed up, took me by the shoulder and asked, "Brother Leo, what has happened?" I promptly answered, "I'm well, I'm healthy!" He knelt down beside me. I myself prayed interiorly: "I love you, though very unworthy, O hidden Lord" and then recited Mary's prayer when Elizabeth praised her, the Magnificat.

After the Bishop had finished blessing the sick and had entered the Rosary Basilica, I rose from my knees without any support and, accompanied by Dr. Jeger, returned to my bed in the Accueil Notre Dame. Our pilgrimage doctors all examined me immediately. They could in no way explain what had just happened and despite my protests told me to stay there. I would have much preferred to go to the Grotto to pray! I prayed and thanked the Lord all through the night without sleeping a wink. I was up at 5 A.M. for Holy Mass in the Accueil Chapel. After Mass Dr. Gruninger of Lucerne came to ask if there were any developments and if I had slept well. "No, I didn't sleep. I spent the night praying and giving thanks. Now I'm hungry. I want something to eat!" The doctor quickly warned me, "It's a long while since you have had a normal meal. You must go carefully, giving your stomach time to readjust!" I replied, "I'm sorry, but I am hungry and need food. The Blessed Virgin does not do things in half

measure!" With that I headed off to the Swiss dining room
and polished off everything I could lay hands on—milk,
coffee, bread, butter, cheese, sausage! I downed enough for
four men and suffered no consequences.

At 8 A.M. they asked me to come to the Medical Bureau.
There were eighteen doctors, presided over by Dr. Francois
Leurat [president of the bureau from 1954]. The doctors
examined and questioned me for four hours, ending at noon.
I was examined again that afternoon. The doctors congratu-
lated me [on my return to full health]. In the course of the
examination I was told what happened: The doctor who
followed directly behind the bishop, and also some sick
people who had been close to me, testified that I had been
projected forcefully out of my wheelchair directly onto my
knees! I did not rise up and kneel; I was ejected onto my
knees! I'm sure it rocked the bishop! I myself knew nothing
of this. I came to consciousness on my knees.

Brother Leo reported to his own doctors immediately on
returning to Fribourg. They found him in perfect health, and
he went straight into full-time work in the monastery. The
next year he returned to Lourdes, carrying signed certificates
from his Swiss doctors. He was reexamined and questioned in
detail by the Lourdes Medical Bureau. No sign of his crippling illnesses was found. As soon as the doctors had finished,
he reported for duty with the stretcher bearers serving the
new sick pilgrims. He repeated this procedure each year.
In 1958, more than six and one-half years after Brother
Leo's cure, the Medical Bureau accepted his case. Professor
Thiebant, in presenting the report, stated that "the circum-
stances of the case remain medically inexplicable".

I mentioned earlier that Dr. Michael Lasalle of the Lourdes
Medical Bureau staff told me in the summer of 1997 that
they have had files on twenty-five hundred "medically inexplicable" cases since the bureau was begun in 1883. (It was
founded by Dr. G. de Saint Maclou, a formidable physician

Brother Leo Schwagger a year after his cure, 1953.

and also a linguist and historian of antiquity. He was actually a baron, descending from ancient Norman aristocracy.) Of course, as Dr. Francis Izard noted in his own book on Lourdes, many people who are cured do not have the wherewithal to keep traveling back yearly for medical examinations by bureau doctors. Izard also pointed out some good cases that have been rejected because the patients' own doctors' original medical certificates were slipshod.

When Brother Leo Schwager's cure was accepted by the Lourdes Bureau in the eighth year after his dramatic healing, his own bishop, Monsignor Charriere of Fribourg-Lausanne, decided to initiate a canonical investigation. In 1908 Pope Pius X, warning against "the word 'miracle' being uttered lightly", had instituted what is called a canonical commission. The usual procedure is this: The bishop of the diocese where the person lives—after the Lourdes Medical Bureau has ruled the case inexplicable to medical science—appoints five persons to reexamine the case. Two of the five must be doctors who are specialists in the disease in question, enjoying renown in that field. They must reexamine the whole history

Brother Leo Schwagger, October 1991.

of the alleged cure. They must decide if the conditions laid down by Pope Benedict XIV in 1734 have been fulfilled.[1] To employ five professional people to go through these steps thoroughly and then publish the results, knowing any unwarranted conclusions will be publicly ridiculed, costs much time and money. Many bishops, believing that generally people will accept the Lourdes Medical Bureau verdict, are not prepared to take all this trouble. That is why there are only sixty-five canonical cures on the books!

On December 18, 1960—eight years and eight months after Brother Leo's cure—his bishop's commission of experts declared the cure miraculous. Monsignor Charriere announced the decision in a pastoral letter to his diocese, calling on prayers of thanksgiving to the Blessed Virgin in each church and chapel.

[1] See page 58.

Brother Leo became an energetic organizer and stretcher-bearer for Lourdes pilgrimages over the next thirty-six years, as an important part of his work. The pilgrims would average thirty-three hundred each time.

On Brother Leo's initial return to Fribourg in 1952, his parish priest said, "Although you now have your health, don't see the cure as a free ticket to heaven!" In 1988, thirty-six years after his cure, he was hospitalized with heart trouble. In 1995 he experienced an internal hemorrhage due to poor coagulation. The same year he suffered a hernia, complicated by painful neuralgia. These problems have in no way made him question God or stopped his going to Lourdes to serve the sick. He remembers that Bernadette, the saint who unearthed the spring of healing water, was never healed of asthma and died of very painful tuberculosis of the bone at age thirty-five. Nuns who nursed her through her many long and painful illnesses—"spitting up whole basins of blood", one remarked—noticed that she never asked for a miracle of healing herself. She said she was content as an invalid, "praying for those who do not pray".[2] She endured weeks of intense agony before her death, and Father Febvre, the chaplain, suggested they would pray for her cure. She responded, "To pray for my cure? Not a bit of it." When Bernadette was in her last and excruciating agony, with hardly any skin left on her back, Mother Eleonore said, "I am going to ask our Immaculate Mother . . . to give you some consolation." Bernadette responded, "No, no consolations, only strength and patience." Brother Leo finds no contradiction in these new sicknesses coming thirty-six years after his cure. Bernadette once said, "Our Lord gives his crown of thorns to his friends."

---

[2] René Laurentin, *Bernadette of Lourdes: A Life Based on Authenticated Documents* (New York: HarperCollins, 1979).

Chapter 6

SERGE PERRIN

"I Went to Learn How to Die"

HENNEBONT IS SITUATED in northwest France, in the region of Brittany. Serge Perrin, of Breton stock, was born there in 1929. The Bretons' deep Christian faith is legendary. The chemist and microbiologist from whom pasteurization gets its name, Louis Pasteur, made this famous remark about Breton faith: "The more scientific truths I discover, the more my faith becomes like that of a Breton peasant." Young Serge grew up with that faith. His father, a permanent army man, taught his eldest child, Serge, order and discipline, which stood him in good stead when he took up the precise profession of accounting. Accountant Perrin prospered and married a local girl, and they were blessed with three children. Things looked very rosy, so they adopted a fourth, a child from Togo. Christianity was a key ingredient of their family life.

Troubles began in February 1964, when Serge woke one day with a headache. He drove twenty-five miles to his office, thinking the pain would pass. As the morning wore on, he began to make uncharacteristic mistakes in his numbers. Then his speech started slurring, and he felt unsteady on his feet. A colleague took him home, and they called the family physician, Dr. Source. The latter diagnosed incomplete hemiplegia (right-side partial paralysis) and referred him to a neurologist in Nevers, Dr. Lefranc. Tests indicated a right upper motor lesion, that is, damage to the nerve-carrying impulses from the central nervous system to the muscles that produce movement. Serge's right leg was especially bad. His right hand and his muscular coordination were also affected, and his cholesterol level was high. Dr. Lefranc frowned when he checked the family history, finding there were many cases of vascular problems. He prescribed a vascular dilator to get the blood flowing freely again and ordered rest from work. The treatment was effective, and three months later Serge was able to return to his office.

Four years later, on December 2, 1968, Serge woke with a severe headache, but, strictly conscientious and disciplined as always, he drove off for work. He had not traveled far when he found his driving becoming erratic. Passing motorists honked or flashed headlights at him angrily. Several times he stopped on the side of the road to pull himself together. He eventually made it to his office but wasn't there long when he collapsed. He was taken home, and Dr. Source was called again. He diagnosed the same problem, but, as it was worse than the previous time, he quickly sent Serge to Dr. Lefranc. Serge was now unable to walk unaided and had trouble forming words, and his blood pressure was 150 over 100. Because the cause was cerebrovascular, the drug sureptil-papaverine was prescribed. This time the patient did not respond. Headaches persisted, there was a worsening in the paralysis of the right leg and arm, and he was losing sight in the left eye.

Three months later, in February 1969, Serge was taken to a neurosurgical clinic in Rennes, where Professor Pecker noted "right-side paralysis affecting the leg chiefly, significant disturbances in superficial and deep sensation and definite reduction of vision in the left eye". Examination by an arterioangiogram indicated the cause was thrombosis (a clot) in the left carotid artery. Surgery would be too risky, so the doctor attempted to remedy the stenosis (constriction of the blood flow) by vascular dilator medication and a low-fat diet. He sent Serge off to an eye specialist, Dr. Drevillon, who confirmed the organic problem in the left eye and "reduction of retinal artery pressure in both eyes, suggesting a bilateral spread of the effects of the thrombosis". Professor Pecker put Serge on an intensive course of the vascular dilator cytochrome. There was no improvement.

The meticulous accountant was used to solving all problems by careful planning and hard work. He was completely thrown off by this life-threatening illness, totally out of his control. Ah, there was Lourdes! His wife agreed enthusiastically to his suggestion of a pilgrimage in May, Mary's month, especially loved by Bretons. He set out for Lourdes with fervent prayers and high hopes but, alas, returned home as bad as before.

In the middle half of 1969, Serge began to have strange episodes of temporary paralysis. He would suddenly lose total muscle control but not consciousness. His doctor was perplexed and very worried by these "cerebral blackouts that must be coming from the blockage in the carotid artery". Serge, the meticulous accountant, kept an accurate record of the increasing attacks of temporary paralysis. By December he was having twelve a month. His distressed wife, never knowing when the next attack would come, tried never to leave him alone.

Medical expenses were piling up, so his wife applied for

government financial assistance. He was examined by Social
Security Department doctors, who classified him "Invalid
Category 3", that is, "completely unable to work and needing
permanent help to survive". He could no longer walk without the assistance of his wife or sticks, his eyesight had
deteriorated remarkably, and there were the increasing episodes of "cerebral blackout".

Eye specialist Dr. Drevillon examined Serge in December.
Distant vision in the left eye was very poor. The field of
vision, that is, what he saw on either side of the object he
focused on, had "contracted almost to a point". It was like
looking down a tunnel.

By January 1970 the paralysis in the right leg and hand had
worsened considerably and had spread to one side of his face.
Professor Pecker commenced intravenous Vincamine treatment and continued it for the next four months—without
interruption, or effectiveness. Serge began having falls as he
shuffled around on his sticks. Never one to hide from reality,
he asked his doctor if he would get better. The physician's
look shook him! Serge asked for an honest estimate of how
long he could last. The reply—"August, maybe"—rocked
him, and panic swept over him. What would happen to his
wife and four children? At age forty, he felt he had hardly
lived. Moods of frustration, anger and semidespair assailed
him. His wife, deeply distressed, suggested another pilgrimage to Lourdes. His emotional response was, he later admitted, "revulsion". He had already been there without the
slightest benefit, and the physical discomfort of the long train
journey would be much worse now. He had trouble getting
words out, but she was left in no doubt. He would not go,
period! Women seem to have reserves of faith and persistence
often lacking in men. She pleaded. Serge, who habitually
found it hard to dodge a good cause, finally agreed to go. But,
he told her, it was only "to learn how to die well".

On the night of April 26, 1970, his wife settled her glum and depressed husband into a couchette on the train carrying the Anjou pilgrims to Lourdes. The long journey proved as trying as he had anticipated. And at Lourdes, as before, he experienced no physical improvement. Then came the last day, May 1. He was terribly tired as his wife wheeled him to the final Mass in the underground Basilica of Pius X— dedicated in 1958 by Cardinal Roncalli, later Pope John XXIII. Huge roof ribs of concrete have created unobstructed space for twenty-thousand worshippers gathered in a circle around an elevated altar. This architectural tour de force was quite lost on the exhausted Serge.

During the anointing of the sick, one of the priests traced the sign of the cross with oil on Serge's forehead, murmuring, "Through this holy anointing may the Lord in his love and mercy help you with the grace of the Holy Spirit." As the priest moved to the invalid lying beside Serge, something began to happen. The thirty-nine-page abbreviated booklet later put out by the Lourdes Medical Bureau explains, "It was at this moment M. Perrin felt a strange warmth in his toes which up to then had felt numb and almost dead. Next he realized his feet were coming back to life, and warmth beginning to spread through his body. He imagined this was caused by the hot water bottles, though normally he could not feel their heat. He lifted the blanket and noticed his right ankle was very swollen. Attributing this to cardiac insufficiency, he thought it was the end! However, the heat spread through his legs, and he stirred in his wheelchair. His wife thought he must want to go to the toilet and asked him to be patient. He replied: 'I don't know what's happened to me but I have the impression I won't need sticks much longer and that I could walk.'" The warming of his body continued for about ten minutes.

As his wife wheeled him back to the hospital after the anointing Mass, Serge lifted the blanket and found his right ankle was its normal size. When he arrived at the hospital, he astounded his wife—and the volunteers who had been observing his debilitated state for almost a week—by stepping out of the wheelchair! Back at his bedside, he told his wife he would not need his sticks anymore and proceeded to walk unaided to the toilet.

Lunchtime came, and some witnesses suggested he use his wheelchair and say nothing, "for the sake of discretion". Could euphoria resulting from all the stirring ceremony, singing and tears on many faces have caused a temporary surge of energy? Lourdes authorities are against any premature dramatizing! After lunch he was wheeled down to the giant Rosary Square for the final procession.

As Serge waited for the thousands of participants to get into position, he absentmindedly took off his glasses and received another thrill. He could see very clearly! He covered his right eye and, with the previously almost-blind left eye, proceeded to read the wording on the banners carried by the different pilgrimage groups. He could even read the signs on the opposite side of the square. The hymns and the crowd's fervent prayers on behalf of the invalids—"Lord, that I may see; Lord, that I may walk"—took on an extraordinary vibrancy for Serge.

The procession over, the Anjou pilgrims went up to the Lourdes station for the journey home. The Perrin family physician, Dr. Sourice, was one of the doctors accompanying the pilgrimage, and word reached him that his terminal patient seemed cured. It was impossible to do a thorough examination on the move but there was no shadow of a doubt about Perrin's eyesight. He was seeing clearly. Perrin then stunned his doctor by leaving the couchette and descending the carriage's steep steps unaided to thank and say farewell to the volunteer helpers on the platform. Then he climbed back into the train and went to his couchette.

The next day, after Serge's peaceful night journey home, Dr. Sourice gave him a very thorough examination in his office. He could find none of the pathological symptoms he had judged fatal just a week before.

Eleven days later, on May 12, Perrin reported to Professor Pecker at his clinic in the city of Rennes. An arteriogram of the aorta showed neither stenosis (artery narrowing) nor thrombosis (clotting) of the left carotid artery. Blood circulated freely. The recovery seemed complete. Pecker did another examination on May 30, with the same result. Similarly, tests by eye specialist Dr. Drevillon found none of the previous abnormalities.

Toward the end of 1973, more than three years after the cure, four doctors acquainted with Serge's medical history did a final painstaking examination of the former patient. It took about two hours and included physical, neurological and psychological testing. Drs. Sourice, Drevillon, Pasquier and Fresnau were a combination competent to cover all three dimensions.

The left eye, which had been very poor, was now perfect. Blood pressure was 135 over 90. Right leg and hand were perfectly mobile. Because critics like the novelist Émile Zola have insisted the Lourdes cures are all "hysterical cases", I shall quote from the psychological assessment signed by the four doctors.

"M. Serge Perrin is an accountant. His care for exact detail is ingrained but is not in any way neurotic. . . . He is calm . . . very much in control of himself . . . shows no signs of mental disorder. . . . He neither dramatized nor appeared self-centered. We detected no signs of anxiety."

As mentioned in Chapter Four, the British War Pensions Office gave John Traynor a full life pension plus a helper's allowance after Turkish machine-gun fire felled him at Gallipoli in 1915. Traynor officially notified the department of his complete cure in 1923, but this was ignored. Some years later Dr. Francis Izard, who met Traynor and wrote about his cure in great detail in his 1938 book on Lourdes, discovered Traynor was still receiving the pension, though now running a lucrative business. With Traynor's permission he wrote to the pensions office, asking to see their medical records on Traynor. His letter also was ignored. The four French doctors who examined Serge Perrin in 1973 discovered that the Nantes branch of Social Security, which had declared Perrin "Invalid, Category 3, completely unable to work", reacted as did the British with Traynor's case. The four doctors were intrigued by the government's reply that "miracles are not listed in the nomenclature of medical conditions".

The doctors' 1973 report also noted that Perrin did twenty hours of accountancy work weekly for the Angers diocesan office and the refuge it runs for the homeless. "He does this work without any fatigue, suffering no more headaches, vertigo, muscular cramps or any parasthesias [tingling] in the limbs. His memory is excellent, as is his speech. He often gives lectures and talks at public meetings, and he drives his car without difficulty day or night. There have been no recurrences of the former attacks."

Dr. Pierre Mouren, professor at the Marseilles Faculty of Medicine and consultant physician of neurology in a number of hospitals in that city, states in the booklet published on the case by the Lourdes Medical Bureau that "M. Serge Perrin's cerebral vascular lesions . . . were cured in a medically inexplicable way." Six years after Perrin's cure, Dr. Dominque Bartoli, consultant ophthalmologist at hospitals in the northeastern French city of Troyes, was asked by the Lourdes Medical Bureau to review the case. He was given the detailed clinical reports compiled by Dr. Source, Professor Pecker and ophthalmologist Dr. Devillon. He gave these conclusions

Serge Perrin back at Lourdes after his cure.
Lourdes Basilica is in the background.

concerning his own special field, diseases of the eye: "My formal verdict is that a serious organic lesion in the optic tract occurred and that it resolved in a quite inexplicable fashion, medically speaking, especially if one takes into account the rapidity of recovery and its virtual 'restitutio ad integrum' [restoration to wholeness]."

Professor Mouren, after stating in writing that he regarded Serge Perrin's recovery inexplicable from a medical standpoint, also noted something one comes across in so many recipients of Lourdes cures—a combination of serenity with an eager readiness to tell anyone interested about the grace received. The professor wrote: "Perrin considers it his duty, even a moral and religious obligation, to inform people about his illness and his cure. One could not but be moved by his final statement about that Anjou pilgrimage to Lourdes." Here is Serge's statement:

> It is a great joy for me and my family, knowing that according to my doctors I should not have lived to see the month of August 1970 because my survival rested on a small four-centimeter (one-and-one-half-inch) artery. But it is also an honor for my parish of Lion d'Angers and our Angers diocese. God, by means of this cure, wished to show how much the anointing rite is more a sacrament of the sick than a sacrament of the dying.
>
> What do the Lord and the Holy Virgin want of me now in return for such a grace? Will I be worthy of what they expect? Whoever you are, whether relatives or friends who read my story, pray for me that I may always bear witness if that is what God and the Holy Virgin require of me.

In the booklet on the Serge Perrin cure, Professor Mouren added, "With Dr. Sourice, who had known Perrin for many years and guaranteed his material and spiritual honesty, we [the team of specialist doctors sent to draft a report for the Lourdes Medical Bureau] were welcomed into a simple, well-kept apartment . . . giving the impression of a united, well-run family home. The conviction that his cure gave him a mission motivated the whole purpose of his life."

Most of us retain some delightful memories from childhood. One I'll never forget is spending nineteen and one-half hours on a slow steam train, sitting on a hard seat, sustained only by doubtful meat pies—with smoke and soot pouring in when we rushed into a tunnel without shutting the windows. Was I a masochist? No, we were going home to Lismore, some 370 miles away from boarding school at Saint Joseph's, Hunter's Hill. It was the term holidays, and we were freed from months of classes, study and institutional cooking. We would crane our necks out the windows for hours, waiting for the first glimpse of "the green, green grass of home".

The first message of Lourdes is that "my Father goes on working, and so do I", as Jesus puts it in John's Gospel. The second: Life is not essentially the search for a comfortable oasis to sit it out beside; life is a journey. The destination, and our real home, if we seek it, is participating in God's beatific life after death has stilled our feet.

An artist's impression of late eighteenth-century Lourdes.

Chapter 7

DR. ALEXIS CARREL

A Nobel Laureate's Unplanned Search for God

THERE USED TO BE a soap with the brand name "Dad". Its advertising line was "Let Dad do it!" I suppose most of us hold nostalgic memories of the sayings and doings of our fathers, which is one reason why the book *Journey to Lourdes*[1] is special to me—the first copy I read was from my dad's bedside library. Dr. Carrel played a prominent part in ending modern scientists' taboo on discussing miracles. His personal religious history also illustrates a key concept about belief in God.

Born in Lyons in 1873, Alexis Carrel suffered the death of his father five years later and came very much under the influence of his mother, a devout believer who later sent him to a local Jesuit school. Early in his university career he was swept off his feet by Kant's *Critique of Pure Reason*. In that book Kant argued, persuasively to Carrel, that it is utterly

[1] Alexis Carrel, *Journey to Lourdes* (London: Hamilton, 1950).

impossible to have any certitude about "causes" of the physical realities that we can see and feel around us. So, for Kant (and Carrel) it is impossible to prove the existence of a Creator-God. It is unclear whether Carrel understood Kant's "ethical argument" for God as the only possible source of morality. Carrel concluded a question-mark God was mainly an archaic academic question, with no real bearing on human life. The human mind cannot penetrate anything beyond the physical world. The only sure pathfinder to the future, Carrel decided, was the scientist, and so he threw himself enthusiastically into medical studies.

Writing of this period later on, he said he became a "tolerant sceptic" but could not resist "smiling at the child-like, fantastic hopes" of his Mass-going mother. While still a university student, he did his year's military service in a French Army alpine unit, which "made complete my scepticism about religion. Our lives could progress quite well without any need of the supernatural." After advanced studies at Dijon University, he returned to Lyons Medical School, where he taught anatomy and conducted research. In 1902, at age twenty-nine, he achieved an international breakthrough, when he became the first to sew together ruptured blood vessels.

Dr. Carrel was unhappy with the "narrow attitude to research" in Lyons and moved to Paris and then to the New World. The year 1906 found him a leading member of the research team at the Rockefeller Institute in New York, a position he would hold until 1939. In 1912 he conducted a successful experiment that startled the world of medical research. He took living tissue from a chicken's heart and kept it alive in a test tube. (In fact, it was kept alive until 1946.) His pioneer work was foundational for present-day surgery on heart and blood vessels and for organ transplants. That year, 1912, he was awarded the Nobel Prize for medicine.

World War I broke out in 1914, and Dr. Carrel immediately took a boat to his endangered France. With the help of the Rockefeller Institute, he set up a laboratory at the Military Hospital in Compiègne. Front-line soldiers were dying or requiring amputations as the result of infected wounds. With an English researcher, Dr. Carrel made an important medical breakthrough, the Carrel Dakin solution for treating deep septic wounds. Its use soon traveled beyond the French battle-fields to become standard medical procedure worldwide.

When the war ended in 1918, Dr. Carrel returned to the Rockefeller Institute in New York, where he and Charles Lindbergh made headlines with the world's first "artificial heart", a mechanical heart pump for use in surgery. In the 1930s, he wrote an extraordinary medico-philosophical book, *Man, the Unknown* (New York: Harper, 1939). It soon became a world bestseller, translated into eighteen languages. It was a prophetic book, warning of wholesale dehumanization and alienation that has now, years later, become obvious to us. Yet it was also a proclamation of hope—provided our race had the discipline to seek the ever-flowing wellsprings of "wisdom".

Herbert Gasser, the new director of the Rockefeller Institute, decided that all staff must retire when sixty-five years old. He made no exception for Dr. Carrel, then age sixty-six. So Dr. Carrel left, reluctantly, in 1939. He and some colleagues had begun planning a new science-morality institute when war broke out in Europe. He sailed to his beloved France and was shocked by the unpreparedness for war, medically and in every way. He returned to the United States to collect funds and medicines.

While Dr. Carrel was still in the United States, France surrendered and was occupied by the Germans. Despite grim warnings from his friends, he left the safety and comfort of America and entered Occupied France via Spain. The Vichy government pressed him to become minister of health. Dr. Carrel refused that offer as well as offers of special food and fuel allowances. He set up an institute in Paris, suffered, with his wife, in an unheated apartment and traveled by bicycle. His health deteriorated.

Dr. Carrel made enemies in Paris by attacking incompetence and irresponsibility in high places. When the Allies liberated Paris in August 1944, someone listed his name as a Nazi collaborator, and newspapers printed the story. He was deeply shocked by this betrayal. Supreme Commander General Eisenhower personally ordered the charges against him to be thrown out. But great harm had been done to Dr. Carrel's morale. He died of a second heart attack on November 5, 1944.

Let us now turn to another Carrel—the young doctor and lecturer who in 1902 found himself launched on an unplanned quest for the ultimate meaning of his life, of every human life. By then an ever-curious researcher, he had been called in on many difficult cases of tuberculosis, a grim reaper in those days before streptomycin. In his hospital rounds, Dr. Carrel had come across several cases of pseudotuberculosis in which the apparent symptoms of TB turned out to have been psychologically induced. His reading of Charcot had previously alerted him to this phenomenon. Pathological mental states can produce pseudosickness that can be cured by psychological methods. When his mother, distressed by his loss of Christian belief, talked of miracle cures at Lourdes, Dr. Carrel was sure these were simply due to Charcot's autosuggestion. He had read *Lourdes*, by the novelist Émile Zola, who reiterated Charcot's explanation of Lourdes cures.

Then he came across the rebuttal of Charcot and Zola by Dr. Gustave Boissarie, who ran the Lourdes Medical Bureau and who was claiming instantaneous physical cures. Dr. Carrel was sure more stringent checking would show all

Boissarie's cases to be psychological. He decided that would be interesting research fieldwork some day.

A doctor acquaintance who had agreed to be part of the medical team accompanying the May 1902 pilgrimage to Lourdes had to back out. Carrel readily agreed to take his place. The result was Carrel's book *Journey to Lourdes*.[2]

The pilgrim train pulled out of Lyons Station at 1 P.M., May 26, 1902. One of the bedridden travelers was Marie Bailly. The sick going on a pilgrimage to Lourdes must carry a detailed medical certificate signed by their own doctor. If a person has a bad turn on the way, the accompanying medical staff will know the appropriate treatment. Marie Bailly's certificate stated that she was in a very advanced stage of tubercular peritonitis, a savage killer in those days.

Her father, Jean-Celestin, an optician, had died of TB at age forty-nine, as had her mother, Elizabeth Girard, at fifty-two, and a brother, twenty-four. Marie herself had developed a dry cough in 1899 at eighteen. When she began to spit blood, she was hospitalized in a TB sanitarium run by the Daughters of Charity at Sainte-les-Lyon, three miles outside Lyons. The TB bacillus in her lungs spread. In 1901 Marie's stomach began to swell; she was eating little and vomiting often. Finally, the sanitarium's Dr. Roy, diagnosing terminal tubercular peritonitis, decided an incision under the umbilicus might prolong her life "just a little" and had her transported to Saint Joseph's Hospital, Lyons, for the operation. Chief surgeon Dr. Goullioux, however, refused to operate,

---

[2] What follows is based on this book, supplemented by research studies on it and on Carrel himself by Dr. Francis Izard and Dom Stanley L. Jaki. (The latter has written around forty books on the relationship between religion and science. In 1987 he was awarded the Templeton Prize, the world's highest award for intellectual endeavor.) I have also used the three chapters on Carrel in *Uncommon Friends* (Harvest Books, 1989), by his close acquaintance James Newton. Finally, some of the materials I have used come from Carrel's *Dossier 54* in the Lourdes Archives.

judging that the operation would surely kill her. He sent her back to the sanitarium. She was in much pain but kept her spirits up. She prayed a lot—especially for a relative, a Lyons journalist who was an atheist. A conviction came to her in prayer that, if she could get to Lourdes, she would be cured—and this relative would then regain his faith in God and in the Gospels. She asked to be included in the coming Lyons pilgrimage. Everyone—Dr. Roy, the nuns and her surviving family—opposed her, saying it was entirely unrealistic and even suicidal. She persisted, however, and finally her family and the nuns, assured by Dr. Roy that she would not live much longer anyhow, agreed.

Gabrielle Goirand, a young nurse who shared Marie's deep faith in Lourdes, volunteered to accompany her. Gabrielle knew the pilgrimage leaders could block patients who were in as critical a condition as Marie, so she used some subterfuge to slip her patient onto the train just before departure. The trip from the hospital had left Marie exhausted and in pain, but as Gabrielle settled her on a mattress stretched over two train seats, Marie gave a wan smile of thanks. The nurse's return smiles faded, however, as the long journey in a jolting carriage began taking a visible toll. By 3 A.M. Marie had become comatose. When the train stopped briefly at a station, Gabrielle raced along the dark platform to Dr. Carrel's compartment and begged his assistance.

Up until this moment Dr. Carrel's diary (later published as the book *Journey to Lourdes*) was full of lively comments about the pilgrim occupants of his carriage and the Maytime beauty of the countryside. When he arrived at Marie's compartment, the tone of his book changed dramatically. Angry at her shocking state, he injected morphine as the nurse filled him in on the young woman's recent medical history. He felt her distended stomach and wrote, "The swelling was apparently caused by solid masses, and there was a pocket of

fluid under her navel. It was classic tubercular peritonitis. . . .
The temperature above normal, legs swollen, heartbeat and
breathing accelerated."

Dr. Carrel could not get back to his compartment until the
train stopped at another station. His mood of disgust that a
critically ill woman was being dragged on a hopeless twenty-
four-hour train journey was not improved when the light of
dawn revealed the other occupants of the compartment—
"two shabby women accompanying their children, one with
a tumor on his knee, the other an idiot girl, fully grown, who
sat there stiffly, grunting like a beast, tongue lolling out of her
mouth". The sunlight flooding the Maytime valleys outside
the window brought into stark contrast "the horrors of this
trainload of sick".

Just before 2 P.M. on May 27 a cheer went up as the Gave,
Lourdes' mountain stream, came into view. Then, wrote
Dr. Carrel, surprised by his changed emotions, "the slender
Lourdes spire, delicate and pure. . . . And from carriage to
carriage sprang up the 'Ave' hymn. . . . No banal tune sung
by chirping girls at church but the Prayer of the Poor."

Volunteer stretcher bearers waiting at the station took
Marie and the other sick to the Hospital of the Seven Sor-
rows. Dr. Carrel was surprised to see a classmate working
among the stretcher bearers. (He did not name him, just
referred to him as "A.B.") Later, when they sat down to
coffee, Dr. Carrel was quick to point out he had not come as
a believer—but to observe and study "the incredible power
of suggestion . . . of an exalted crowd bonded in prayer. . . .
There can be enormous effects on the nervous system but
absolutely none on organic diseases." A.B. retorted spiritedly,
quoting some documented cases of instantaneous organic
healings. The de Rudder case is a classic, he added. (I have
treated this in a later chapter.) Dr. Carrel countered, "Pious
propaganda, lacking objective, scientific investigation! . . . If

the de Rudder case was scientifically authenticated it would be an archetypal miracle, God's signature, supernatural. . . . It is my duty to approach such cases with complete scepticism. . . . Charcot has demonstrated how paralysis and arthritis, formerly judged to be incurable conditions, may really be nervous diseases which can be cured instantaneously. . . . Such remission will occur here, but not cures of truly organic sicknesses . . . like that of the patient Marie in my care. . . . She has tubercular sores, lesions of the lungs and for the last eight months peritonitis diagnosed by a well-known surgeon from Bordeaux. . . . She may die at any moment. . . . If she were cured I'd never doubt again; I'd become a monk!" A.B. laughed but warned Carrel about making rash promises.

Dr. Carrel returned to the hospital and asked Marie how she felt. She looked with "dim, dark circled eyes. Her colourless lips moved in a soundless reply. . . . Her pulse was 150 [beats] to the minute and irregular. . . . Solid masses still in her distended stomach . . . legs swollen . . . nose and hands become cold . . . ears and nails with a bluish tinge." A physician from a town near Bordeaux walked in, and Dr. Carrel asked his assessment. After a careful examination he whispered, "She's at the point of death." Dr. Carrel went over to the nun in charge, telling her it would be quite irresponsible to have Marie taken to the Grotto baths and the procession for the sick. The nun shook her head firmly: It would be wrong to refuse the poor girl her dying wish.

They took Marie by stretcher to the Grotto, Nurse Goirand shielding her with a sun parasol. Dr. Carrel gazed at the pitiful collection of pathologically hopeless cases and was swept with "a strange and novel emotion . . . and a longing to believe with these unfortunates that the Virgin Mary was not merely a charming creation of human imagination". He found himself "praying for Marie, who had suffered unimaginably, asking the Virgin to restore life to her and faith to himself". But that "exultation" did not survive long. He forced himself back to "the sure road of orderly scientific search, determining to be wholly objective".

Nurse Goirand accompanied Marie into the women's bath cubicles. They soon emerged, the nurse explaining that her patient looked so spent they decided not to immerse her but just to pour water on her swollen stomach. Dr. Carrel jotted down the time in his notebook: 2:20 P.M.

Marie and other stretcher cases were carried to the nearby Grotto and lowered to the ground. Marie was up front, the blanket over her shaped by the mound in her stomach, which was as big as that of a very pregnant woman. A young priest faced the sick and the crowd behind them and began praying aloud. They joined in enthusiastically, repeating his invocations, "Holy Virgin, heal our sick. . . . Jesus, we love you." He held his arms like Christ on the Cross, and many followed suit. Dr. Carrel commented that emotion swept the crowd, "lashing them like a mountain storm". He studied the faces of the sick he recognized, "especially the faces of the neurosthentics, expecting to see those nervous cases rise from their stretchers and joyfully claim a healing. But none stirred." That disappointed him. He had hoped, given the intensity of the prayer, to see a case or two of "cures" generated by autosuggestion and religious hysteria.

He moved beside Marie's stretcher and noted color had returned to her face, and her breathing was slower and more regular. He jotted down the time, 2:40 P.M., and "concentrated all powers of observation on her. . . . Her appearance was definitely changing." The eyes, so dull before, were now wide open and gazed "ecstatically" at the Grotto. Dr. Carrel's notes recorded another extraordinary change: "2:55 P.M., stomach swelling seems to be flattening. 3:10, breathing forty per minute, heartbeat definitely stronger. Says she is feeling better. 3:20, no sign of stomach distension—blanket flattened out! When questioned she replies, 'I am still weak but feel I am cured.'" Dr. Carrel adds that his "mind was in a blank, a feeling of going mad!"

Stretcher bearers took Marie back to the hospital. Dr. Carrel went to see Dr. Boissarie, who "showed no trace of surprise" at his story. The director of the Medical Bureau added that if Marie's case was genuine, it would not be the first tubercular peritonitis cure. Should Dr. Carrel wish to, he was told, he could read the Father Salvator case in the Medical Bureau files.

Father Salvator, a Capuchin priest, contracted pulmonary (lung) tuberculosis in 1898, at age thirty-six. Two years later his doctors told his superior he was dying of tubercular peritonitis, and further treatment was completely pointless. When told this, Father Salvator said he would go on pilgrimage to Lourdes, to the voiced opposition of his doctors. It was a long and painful train journey from Dinard in Brittany. He arrived at Lourdes in a shocking state on June 26 and was taken immediately to the baths. He emerged so "rejuvenated that neither he nor those with him could doubt his cure", states the official Medical Bureau report. He ate a hearty meal that night and was examined at the Medical Bureau the next day. All signs of TB had disappeared. Medical checkups over the next eight years found absolutely no sign of the disease. He went to work in Rennes, where Archbishop Dubourg, having studied the Lourdes Medical Bureau findings, set up a commission of theologians and doctors to review the case. The latter ruled that this "instantaneous, radical and definitive cure of a grave organic disease" was medically inexplicable. On July 1, 1908, the archbishop's commission accepted Father Salvator's cure as miraculous. It is number twenty-six in the list of canonical cures—that is, those officially investigated and accepted by Church authorities after having been passed by the Lourdes Medical Bureau. The 1998 president of

Fr. Salvator, age 38, cured of virulent TB, Lourdes, June 25, 1900.

the bureau, Dr. Théodore Mangiapan, wrote in the preface to a book detailing the sixty-five canonical cures, "All the [Lourdes] cures could not be included in this [canonical] list. That would require an encyclopedia! And even then it would almost certainly have been incomplete."

But back to the sequence of events recorded in Dr. Carrel's notes on the very day of Marie Bailly's cure. Accepting—perhaps hoping for?—the possibility that the extraordinary physical change might be merely a temporary psychosomatic phenomenon "due to the religious fervor at the Grotto" he went to her hospital at 7:30 P.M., "tense and burning with curiosity". Passing rows of sick who had attended the ceremonies with Marie but who had not been cured, he was surprised at "the happiness on their faces". He had expected them to be dejected and even resentful.

When he reached Marie's bed, she was sitting up "with bright eyes and glowing with vitality . . . such inexpressible serenity flowed from her that it seemed to light up this pathological place with joy". Her pulse beat regularly at eighty beats per minute. Then, "torn between hope and fear", he threw back the covering to find "above the narrow hips the small, flat, slightly concave abdomen of a young, undernourished girl". He could "palpate her stomach without causing her pain. All traces of the distension and the hard masses were gone. They had vanished like a bad dream. . . . Only the legs were still swollen." He realized he was perspiring and his heart was beating furiously.

He invited the two doctors who had examined her with him before the cure to do so again. They did and agreed that the unmistakable condition of terminal tubercular peritonitis had disappeared. An Italian doctor stood close by. He was a recent convert to Catholicism and said to Dr. Carrel, "It's a miracle all right. I've been praying for you, Doctor. Maybe this will bring you to belief." Dr. Carrel writes that he said nothing in reply. He was "completely confused".

A second shock was in store. He turned to the beaming young woman "who had been rescued from misery to light, to freedom . . . to life itself". He was sure she would be in a full flood of excitement about future plans, no doubt including marriage and a family, that just twenty-four hours ago were a cruel impossibility. Sharing in the excitement on her face, he asked, "What will you do now that you are cured?"

"I shall join the Sisters of Saint Vincent de Paul and nurse the sick", she replied. These nuns, also called the Daughters of Charity, were the ones who had looked after her in the sanitarium outside Lyons. Carrel, to whom the satisfaction of worldly success and recognition was essential to happiness, was thunderstruck by her decision to sacrifice her life for other sick. To hide his emotions he left the room.

Needing to be alone to calm his racing thoughts and feelings, he left the town for the quiet beyond the Grotto, where the only sounds came from the woods and the swiftly flowing river. The nightly torchlight procession had begun, and he could hear "the full-throated, discordant voices of the crowd singing over and over, and with ascending enthusiasm, the 'Ave Ave' chorus of the Lourdes hymn". While feeling no inclination to join them, he "no longer wanted to smile patronizingly at their fantastic hopes".

Just beyond the Grotto the light from a cluster of tall votive candles revealed his schoolmate A.B., who had also sought out a quiet place. He greeted Dr. Carrel warmly. "Are you convinced at last, doubting philosopher?" he asked. That was a challenge Carrel was not yet ready for, and he replied sharply, "A scientist can't readily accept unseen causes like your Supernatural. How can I be absolutely certain it was not pseudoperitonitis?" "Come on, now", said his friend. "Just yesterday you took her as an example of a perfectly organic disease. Ready to become a monk if she was cured!"

"A rash promise, I admit, but all it proves is my honest belief, not my scientific inaccuracy", said Dr. Carrel. "It is possible I erred in my medical judgment, you know." A.B. replied that even if, for the sake of hypothesis, it was pseudo-tuberculosis, how could he explain the instantaneous nature of the cure? Had Dr. Carrel ever seen in his wide medical experience such a speedy disappearance of such extraordinary symptoms? Carrel agreed A.B. had a point. He also admitted that the dismissal of Lourdes cures as "mere hysteria and autosuggestion" did not seem very convincing in the light of this Marie Bailly case. "There seems to be some extraordinary energy in Lourdes water which must be investigated", he added. A.B. retorted, "But what about the cures of people praying to Our Lady of Lourdes far away from here, like Pierre de Rudder at the shrine in Belgium? The

Medical Bureau will show you the papers signed by doctors who were directly involved with de Rudder."

"I'll grant you this", replied Dr. Carrel. "It will be simple justice to let the medical world know that stupendous healings do take place here. I will inform my Lyons colleagues. It is most imperative that a medical commission come here to discover what is happening."

If mere "autosuggestion" were the explanation, Dr. Carrel mused, we would be seeing similar instantaneous healings elsewhere. He himself had treated some cases of psychologically induced illness but he had never seen an instantaneous disappearance like Marie Bailly's. A.B. was no one's fool, nor was Boissarie, and they were claiming there were many such cures here. A.B. interrupted Dr. Carrel's reverie, explaining that his stretcher work began early next morning, so he must return to his lodging. He left Dr. Carrel with a hint: "De Rudder was cured when he prayed. . . ."

The next five pages of Dr. Carrel's *Journey to Lourdes* portray his agitated efforts to reach a decision. Now it was midnight, and he found himself "a solitary, troubled human, wrestling in the dark with scientific doubts and questionings". As he reviewed the extraordinary turn of events, his mind struggled like a swimmer in a swirling surf. Yes, "it was distressingly uncomfortable to be personally involved in a miracle"—despite his earlier confidence when he told A.B. he was unafraid of what he might discover in his research at Lourdes. That was his habitual mindset in his Lyons laboratory. Was Lourdes a laboratory and its cures researchable scientifically? Or did it belong to a completely new world, above and beyond scientific grasp? In other words, was the supernatural world as real as the natural? Did God really exist, a Person consciously at work beyond yet within phenomena? Was Lourdes at the cutting edge of the meaning of human life and death . . . and after death?

His "conflict of soul would not cease. There was no way of proving God did not exist or that the Virgin was not merely an imaginary figment. Neither could be proved or denied." An epoch-creating scientist, Pasteur had died just five years before, a man so sure of his Christian beliefs that he relished public debates with unbelievers. What made Pasteur sure, Dr. Carrel wondered to himself, that he had bridged the chasm between science and the supernatural?

Dr. Carrel reviewed what he had seen happen to Marie Bailly. She was not even immersed in the Lourdes water. A.B. confidently claimed that de Rudder's shattered leg was healed instantaneously six hundred miles from Lourdes, as he prayed alone at a replica shrine. Prayed! Did "a vast crowd at fervent prayer release a natural force as yet unknown"?

About 2 A.M. Dr. Carrel walked past the Grotto into the wide piazza in front of the basilica, "restless and distressed". He was startled to hear loud singing from the basilica at such a late hour. He climbed the steps and stood at the church entrance and longed to "come to a conclusion. The diagnosis had been quite certain; an undeniable miracle had taken place." But how could he know the "miracle" was caused by "God"? Yes, put off any conclusion, any decision! Some time in the future he might have enough evidence to make a sure judgment. No hasty decisions now! And yet . . .

He entered the basilica, which was ablaze with lights and candles and resonating with one thousand Basque voices, and seated himself at the back. Covering his face with his hands, he wrote, he listened intently to the singing. Gradually he found himself doing what the pilgrims were doing, what A.B. hinted he must do to discover the truths beyond phenomena. He found himself praying and admitting that he was "an uneasy sinner . . . troubled in spirit and exhausted from the proud pursuit of vanities". (He wrote these things as a personal account, not intended for publication. Only after his death did his wife publish it in the book *Journey to Lourdes*.)

At this point Dr. Carrel abandoned his scientific positivism, his agnosticism, and unashamedly prayed, and prayed like a Romanticist! He found it easier to pray to Mary: "Gentle Virgin, who aid the troubled who turn to you. . . . I believe in you. You answered my petition with a blazing miracle. But I still cannot see; I still doubt. But my deepest yearning is to believe, passionately, totally, never more analyzing and doubting." He ended up his prayer reverie: "Beneath the deep, harsh warnings of intellectual pride a smothered dream persists. Alas, it is still only a dream, but the most enchanting dream of all—the dream of believing in and loving you with the shining spirit of the men of God."

He walked back to the hotel "absorbed in prayer", an almost forgotten experience. Seated at the dressing table, he took out his big green notebook and wrote up the events of the momentous day, finishing when it was almost dawn. He closed the notebook and had, he thought, closed the door on doubt. In that tranquil moment of first light of day "all the worries of daily life, of hypotheses, conjectures and mental doubts had disappeared". Carrel decided he had found "certitude". But not for long, as we shall see!

A little later that same morning, Thursday, May 29, 1902, Marie Bailly woke refreshed, dressed herself and attended Mass. After being granted the request to be fully immersed in the famous baths, she was escorted to the Medical Bureau. Dr. Boissarie and other doctors, including Carrel, examined her. They wrote depositions stating they could find no traces of the physical disease that had, according to her own doctor's reports, grown progressively worse over the last four years. Immediately following Dr. Carrel's statement was that of Dr. Paul Geoffray of Rive de Gier, Loire. He wrote that he had seen Marie Bailly the day before "in a state of total prostration . . . a huge hard mass in her stomach . . . indicating imminent death". Having described the changes when he examined her several hours after she returned from the prayers at the Grotto, he concluded, "Should I add to this signed statement that tubercular peritonitis has never been cured in several hours, as has happened in this case."

The exuberant Marie told Dr. Carrel she would now go straight back to Lyons. He tried to dissuade her: A train trip of more than twenty-four hours could cause serious physical distress, given her still-emaciated state. She kept her own counsel, took the train and staggered her family. She simply took a streetcar from Lyons Station and walked in on them unannounced. The next day she boarded the streetcar again and walked the considerable distance from the stop to report in "to the nuns who had nursed me with such care".

Dr. Roy, who had opposed her Lourdes journey as suicidal, looked at the still-emaciated Marie and privately told a colleague that it could be only a temporary arrest of the disease due to religious "hysteria". He insisted she be put to bed again in the sanitarium, monitored her daily and was bewildered to see her putting on almost two pounds per week. Six weeks later, on July 15, he wrote, "The cure seems complete." The doctor added that her psychological state was quite normal.

On November 27 Dr. Carrel interviewed Marie and wrote down in greater detail the story of her four years' progressive illness, her experiences at Lourdes and her present state of health. The next day Marie left for Paris to join the Rue du Bac Convent of the Daughters of Charity. Dr. Carrel was allowed to visit her there periodically to take blood and urine tests. The results of these, which he sent to Dr. Boissarie and which are still in the file at Lourdes, were completely TB negative. Dr. Carrel also stressed the physical and psychological rigors of Rue du Bac's life. Marie and her convent companions rose at 4 A.M. for an hour of meditation followed by Mass. After breakfast there was a lecture on spirituality and then study. After that came the heavy physical work, required to keep the large community near to self-supporting, in vegetable gardens, the kitchen, and so on. Marie worked in the laundry, no light task in those days before washing machines and electric irons. Dr. Carrel noted Marie had no difficulty in keeping up with the sturdy novices who came from farming households. She survived the tough novitiate with excellent health, took her vows and lived as a Daughter of Charity until she died in 1937. Her health was never a problem. Daughters of Charity in that era worked above all for the impoverished, especially in city slums. Their lives were certainly austere.

Now back to Dr. Carrel: In June 1902 he returned from Lourdes to his laboratory in Lyons University. He was excited and keen to share his extraordinary findings. An opportunity soon came at a meeting attended by the principal members of the university's medical faculty. After giving an enthusiastic account of the Marie Bailly case, he concluded, "There is something here which approaches the category of the miraculous." Then followed, he later related, "a chilling silence" in response. Dr. Carrel continued, suddenly defensive: "I would like to inform you I saw the patient again this morning. She is perfectly cured." "Cured?" one doctor interjected. Another added, "With such notions you seem to be entertaining, Dr. Carrel, I believe it is my duty to inform you that we have no place for you here." Dr. Carrel was stunned and angry, so much so that he soon resigned from the university and went to work in Paris—where he found similar hostility to any talk of Lourdes cures. In 1904 he set sail for North America. There is no record of his former colleagues' reaction when he won the Nobel Prize for medical research eight years later!

Something else happened in Lyons just after Dr. Carrel's angry confrontation with the university medical faculty, and this also upset him very much. Marie Bailly, as was noted, went to Lourdes believing God would cure her and thereby bring her journalist relative, an atheist, to belief. When a reporter came to see her within days of her return, she related her Lourdes experience enthusiastically, giving a full account and naming Dr. Carrel as the foremost medical witness of her miracle. The *Le Nouvelliste* article appeared on June 8, less than a fortnight after Marie's cure, and was unfortunately intemperate and aggressive. Its concluding sentence misrepresented the doctor's: "Unless they want to incur the guilt of bad faith, they must accept the Bailly case as a miracle." The Lourdes Medical Bureau would deny that claim of a miracle as premature—there had to be a lengthy time lapse, usually some years, before they accepted a cure as permanent and therefore possibly miraculous.

In 1902 France was a bitterly divided nation. Catholicism was a "sign of contradiction", evoking passions for and against. Before the 1789 French Revolution, Catholicism, though deeply divided internally, was shored up by royal privileges. Many bishops were aristocrats out of touch with the masses. The latter turned their fury on the Church during the Revolution—and on revolutionary compatriots over the next decade—as fear and suspicion bred violence and counterviolence. Catholic leadership, still at a low ebb intellectually and low on morale after the Revolution, was propped up again by deeply resented imperial favors during the reign of Napoleon III, 1852–1870. The anti-Catholic Republicans exacted vengeance when the Prussian Army ended his rule and the monarchy. The Republicans regarded Catholics as obscurantist enemies of the new scientific progress and democracy—and highly dangerous because of all the schools they ran. Through a series of laws the new

leaders expelled most religious orders from France and confiscated the schools, monasteries and convents. Catholics appeared to the majority Republicans as seditiously working
for a restoration of the monarchy and the *ancien regime*. The
French Church, already weakened by infighting over Jan-
senism, Gallicanism and Quietism, was seen and hated as
obsolete and an obstacle to social happiness.

Now the widely read article in *Le Nouvelliste*, which had
misquoted Dr. Carrel, trumpeted that he was a Catholic
convert. That he resented fiercely. Intensely devoted to independence of thought, he suddenly became guarded and suspicious of being manipulated because of his Lourdes journey.
He had *Le Nouvelliste* print his response to the article. In it he
lamented the fanaticism and blindness on both sides of the
religious divide and the way party politics and selective presentation leave people confused. While suggesting that scientists may one day discover forces in nature accounting for
apparently supernatural phenomena like Lourdes miracles, he
attacked scientists who dismiss Lourdes claims without investigating what actually happens there.

He left Lyons and went to continue his medical research
work in Paris. There he came under the influence of the
Jewish philosopher Henri Bergson, who was drawing large
crowds to his classes at Collège de France. The professor,
who, like Carrel, would later become a Nobel Prize winner,
was attacking the "exaggerated scientism and mechanistic
evolutionism" of the scientists—such as, mused Dr. Carrel, in
his own Lyons University Medical School! Bergson saw great
dangers in their neglect of the spiritual part of man, in their
smugness at dominating and not reverencing nature. Pointing
to the *élan vital* in nature and people, Bergson saw God as the
Source. For him "saints and mystics" were "the great heroes".
Dr. Carrel decided Bergson was worth a serious hearing.

Finding scientific Paris just as narrow as Lyons, Dr. Carrel decided to embark for the New World in 1904. As was noted earlier, he became a medical research scientist at New York's Rockefeller Institute. Though wary of organized religion, he continued to ponder the significance of what was happening at Lourdes. He returned there in 1909 and 1910. During the 1910 visit, he actually witnessed another stunning "miracle"—an eighteen-month-old child blind from birth suddenly restored to sight. The nurse holding the child at the time was Anne de la Motte. She used to volunteer her services yearly to help sick pilgrims at Lourdes. Dr. Carrel, in obtaining all the details on the child from her, became well acquainted with her; in fact, he married her on December 26, 1913! She became his valued research assistant and published some of his manuscripts after his death. Her deep prayer life was later to become a factor in his spiritual research.

Dr. Carrel visited Lourdes again in 1911 and, returning from receiving the Nobel Prize in Stockholm, again in 1912. He was certainly in Lourdes again in 1930—he was one of the doctors who signed the Medical Bureau dossier on a Belgian woman, Marguerite Adam. She had been suddenly cured of TB in both lungs at Lourdes the year before, and now, twelve months later, was completely free of any symptoms of TB.

In 1931, Alexis Carrel was awarded the Sophie Nordhoffe-Jung Cancer Prize. In 1935 he published his international bestseller *Man, the Unknown*. When a French publisher rejected it—"It is magnificent, but there aren't fifty people in France who would read it"—Carrel took it to Harper's. Very quickly it sold a million copies, and it was later translated into nineteen languages! What was the secret of its popularity? Maybe this: Dr. Carrel spelled out very clearly what many were beginning to see—the ominous cracks in the foundations of the "modern scientific culture". He pointed to, for instance, problems that would galvanize the environmental movement some decades later—"Polluted air in cities . . . soil exhausted by chemical fertilizers . . . adulterated food . . . destruction of natural beauty". He foresaw human catastrophes being spawned by a wholesale "indifference to all except money", which was even corrupting supposedly responsible leaders such as judges and politicians. Young Carrel had seen scientists as the modern pathfinders to humanism and happiness. Now, however, he saw an increasing number motivated solely by "what leads to the greatest comfort and convenience", rather than by "the higher interests of humanity". So many scientists had unthinkingly accepted, he continued, the childish dogma of "a mechanistic, physico-chemical conception of life", which would lead inevitably to "mediocrity of goal and narrowness". The new breed, the psychologists and psychoanalysts, vaunted a "confidence that is illusory. . . [as] insanity increases in society". Freud did great harm because his findings were accepted as universal principles instead of "observations about chiefly sick people". Moderns were beginning to "reject all discipline of their appetites . . . leading to selfishness, irresponsibility and dispersion. . . . They degenerate individually and as a race." All this was leading to "the break-up of families, decrease in moral fibre . . . precocious corruption of children . . . a return to barbarism in advanced, scientific nations". (How close to the bone is the last remark, in view of what Hitler and Stalin were brewing while the democracies laughed and played!) Alienating forces were at work, he lamented: "Man has become a stranger in the world he has created."

History, he continued, shows that some "solitude" is essential for "great thinking". Our now invasive media, however, fill the atmosphere with noise and cheap entertainment, leaving people "restless and disordered" and society burdened by "gloom and vulgarity".

He felt sure that Western civilization was more robust

"when religion was the basis of family and social life". He laid much of the blame also at the feet of modern churchmen who taught a religion that is "too rational" and quite deficient in deep prayer. Recalling what Bergson wrote about the essential role in human history of saints and true contemplatives, Dr. Carrel said that real prayer leads to "inner strength, light, love, ineffable peace. . . . Mysticism is splendidly generous . . . bringing the fulfillment of the highest human ideals." Noting that "discipline and unself-centeredness" are prerequisites for this deep prayer, he saw that "the rich and powerful" find it hard to pray deeply, while "the simple seem to feel God as easily as the heat of the sun or the kindness of a friend." A careful reading of *Man, the Unknown* and of what friends have written about the Carrel of 1935 indicates he was confessing his own inability for "deep prayer"—his wife, for instance, still attended Mass alone. He had certainly developed an intense (and personally frustrating) interest in the God question, but his was essentially a purely intellectual quest—as was evident in his discussions with the philosophers Bergson, Sertillanges and Maritain. Very honest discussions they were, but within the rigid parameters of human philosophy. He was forgetting that he criticized churchmen for being "too rational" and deficient in prayer.

In the summer of 1937, while summering at his tranquil and beloved island of Saint Gildas on the Breton coast, he had an invitation to meet a Francis of Assisi–like monk, the Cistercian Dom Alexis Presse. Dr. Carrel was at first reluctant, but, urged strongly by his wife, he went to meet Presse "against his better judgment". The monk told him bluntly that philosophical discussion would not bridge the gulf between us and the Absolute One. "Love is the only way of discovering the real God", he said. Carrel came away saying, "I have met a genuine saint." He multiplied opportunities to speak with Presse and noted that Presse did not just theorize

Alexis Carrel (right) with Charles Lindbergh,
Time *magazine cover, June 13, 1938.*

about "deep prayer" but did it. Dr. Carrel now had a flesh-and-blood "mystic" as a friend.

Some American philanthropists, impressed by a worldwide audience for *Man, the Unknown*'s trenchant criticism of the modern West, offered to raise the sum of several million dollars for Dr. Carrel to set up an "Institute for Man", a place of scientific-spiritual research for a better human future. While they were debating its location, Nazi Germany attacked Dr. Carrel's motherland. He decided to return to France.

Dr. Carrel continued his plans to set up his Institute for Man, which he saw as all the more necessary in a Nazi-controlled Europe. His warning in *Man, the Unknown* about the increasing "barbarism in modern scientific nations" was no longer theoretical! He seized every opportunity to talk with the ascetic Cistercian Dom Presse, a man for whom prayer was an energizing activity rather than a theoretical possibility. One of Carrel's diary entries, dated only "1942", when living conditions were bleak, reads, "I believe in the existence of God, the immortality of the soul, in Revelation and in all the Catholic Church teaches, including the admirable doctrine of sacrifice, which is its very core." In a historical survey in *Man, the Unknown*, he had noted that "sacrifice seems to be a necessary condition of progress" and added that "sacrifice is not difficult when inspired by a high purpose and vast horizons . . . when one burns with a passion for a great adventure." He lamented the lack of such vision and spiritual dynamism in many scientists and intellectuals he knew.

He now believed revelation, that is, the Bible. In Matthew 16, when Simon Peter first confessed Jesus is "the Christ, the Son of the living God", Jesus replied, "Blessed are you, Simon Bar-Jonah! For flesh and blood has not revealed this to you, but my Father who is in heaven." Flesh and blood, that is, merely human thinking, cannot grasp the Absolute, the

Infinite. But God will enter the heart of the true seeker, the one who prays humbly and earnestly, with "revelation", which brings the gift of faith. The Bible rephrases this often in urging us to have the heart of a child.

Paul repeated this theme in 1 Corinthians 2: One cannot receive the revelation of the Holy Spirit by mere human philosophy—of which the Greek Corinthians were understandably proud, given Socrates, Plato and Aristotle! The Holy Spirit, he continued, reveals realities beyond the human mind. Dr. Carrel's compatriot, the great scientist Blaise Pascal, had insisted on the need for humble and prayerful seeking if one wishes to meet God. You meet him in your deepest faculty, the spirit or heart, he pointed out. Dag Hammarskjöld, second secretary general of the United Nations, wrote of his long search for ultimate reality in his posthumously published diary, *Markings*. When he finally came to belief in God in 1953, the diary became filled with quotations from great mystics and masters of prayer—and from the Psalms (which is the Bible at prayer). Three times he quoted Saint John of the Cross: "Faith is the marriage of God and the soul." A real marriage is essentially about fulfilling experiences of the heart, the spirit, rather than the mind's ideas!

Dr. Carrel was deeply distressed by inefficiency, time serving and self-seeking among government and medical officials. Never one to avoid confrontation over irresponsibility—above all when his homeland was at stake—he told people off and made enemies. The mental tension, inadequate food and poor living conditions took a toll on Alexis Carrel's health. Just before Paris was liberated in August 1944, he suffered a heart attack. A few months later he suffered a more serious heart attack. For some time he had been attending Mass as a believer, and now he requested the sacrament of anointing. Some days before he died, he said to Monsignor Hamoyon, "When one approaches one's own death, one grasps the nothingness of all things. I have gained fame. The world speaks of me and my achievements. Yet I am a mere child before God, and a poor child at that!"

Word was sent to Dom Alexis that Dr. Carrel was dying, and he made the long journey to his friend's bedside on a freight train. He was with him on November 5, 1944, when heart disease killed the man whose pioneer work had given new life to many heart patients.

Dr. Carrel personally witnessed two Lourdes miracles. As late as 1940 he was still thinking some scientific break-throughs might provide a natural explanation. Pascal in *Pensées* has advice about "going down on your knees" if you want authentic answers to God questions. Alexis Carrel eventually did just that. Consider Psalm 131: "My heart is not lifted up, my eyes not raised too high. I do not occupy myself with things too great." The psalmist rejects the earlier propensity to venture into the mysterious ways of God as though to understand and control them.

The author of Psalm 131 was not unlike Alexis Carrel. He set out with supreme confidence in his mental powers to solve the mysteries of life. But he came back to trust in the God of revelation of whom his mother had taught him.

Chapter 8

HEALING OF SMALL CHILDREN

THE PHOENICIANS believed that thunder was the voice of the god Baal and lightning his fiery javelins that split the clouds to bring rain. Such "miracles" grew fewer as scientists appeared. The medical scientist Jean Charcot (1825–1893) demonstrated that some afflictions, such as paralysis, could be of nervous origin. He concluded that the paralysis of the vasomotor nerves of Demoiselle Corin was of obvious hysterical origin, and so her cure in Paris at the tomb of Deacon Francis was not a miracle. Charcot, without actually studying them, categorized all Lourdes miracles as merely psychological, due to what he derisively termed "faith healing". Such a decision, made from afar, is not quite scientific!

Charcot, however, makes a valid point. Common sense tells us to look for natural explanations first when confronted with unaccustomed phenomena. Medical doctors see many cases of recoveries that excite lay folk but are due to nervous factors similar to cases Charcot discusses. Even adult minds and nervous systems can play strange tricks at times. This is why the cures of infants at Lourdes are of special interest. They are not susceptible to adult psychological influences.

The Protestant researcher Ruth Cranston understood this. In her book on Lourdes miracles she gave twenty pages to four cases of children. For example, Gerard Baille became blind at the age of two. Six years later, on September 26, 1947, he was taken from the Arras Institute for sightless children to Lourdes. As his mother led him along the Way of the Cross, he suddenly looked up at her and said, "Oh, Mama, how beautiful you are." When the overjoyed parents took him to oculist Dr. Camps at Tarbes, the stunned verdict was, "Gerard had a bilateral chorioretinitis, with double optic atrophy. He cannot—or should not—see!" Yet he saw and still does. He left the Arras Institute for the blind and went to a normal school at Dunkerque, where he won accolades for his academic achievements.

Ruth Cranston searched out Yves Joucau and his parents in their Montmartre home in Paris. The parents told of their grief when their only child, Yves, came down with spinal problems, at age seven. The family doctor sent him to a specialist, who X-rayed him and had him admitted to the hospital immediately. Two bones in the neck had already disintegrated—which explained why his head kept bending to the side. Dr. Leveuf broke the news to his parents. The child had tuberculosis of the vertebrae, or Pott's disease, and must be put into a plaster cast for two to three years. And after that? The doctors shrugged. Upon being questioned, they admitted he might become completely paralyzed.

The parents had little money (like so many of those favored with a Lourdes cure!), but they took the boy to Lourdes. The mother told Cranston of returning to their hotel after the procession of the Blessed Sacrament and suddenly discovering Yves was a changed boy. He wanted to eat, to play, to do things he had not done for months. She supplied the original reports from Hospital Bretonne stating the boy had Pott's disease. Six months later the same hospital issued a complete clearance. The mother showed that report, too. Yves has grown up to be a good athlete, the mother added. The family repeats the Lourdes journey every August, the month he was healed.

Because Lourdes is in France, a large proportion of pilgrims and of the cured are French. Cranston spoke French fluently and visited many of the miracle cases she researched. One of these was Guy Leydet, living in Saint-Etienne, about thirty miles southwest of Lyons. He was a healthy child until, at age five, he was stricken with meningo-encephalitis, a brain disease that ruins the nervous system. It left the boy subject to frequent epileptic fits, incontinent and severely brain damaged, with paralyzed arms and legs. He could neither recognize his mother nor feed himself. It nearly broke her heart to hear nothing but animal-like guttural sounds instead of his once-lovely voice.

For two years his middle-class parents spent a small fortune, willingly paying for any treatment that might cure him or even improve his pitiful condition. Nothing helped, and the doctors finally told them that medical science had exhausted all possibilities.

On October 6, 1946, the mother carried the emotionless seven-year-old into the *piscines*, the baths, while the father knelt outside in desperate prayer. The mother helped the volunteer nurses undress the rigid body and lower it into the water. She feared the chill mountain water—usually about fifty-five degrees Fahrenheit—might bring on another fit.

Instead, Guy opened his eyes and looked around intelligently, "as he used to when he would wake up before his sickness", related the mother. Then he reached out his arms for her, "calling Mama in a sweet voice and began to chatter". She threw clothes over him and raced him out to her husband. Over the next several days of the pilgrimage they marveled as his reawakened intelligence and speech began to make up for the lost two years. His useless arms and legs moved freely once more.

Upon returning to Saint-Etienne they took him to their doctor, who was dumbfounded. Within a year Guy had caught up with children his own age.

One year later, on September 26, 1947, the parents presented him, with certificates from doctors who had treated him during his illness, to the Lourdes Medical Bureau. Forty doctors watched a Paris pediatrician, Dr. Dailly, put Guy through two hours of classical tests. He concluded the examination with the statement "This child is normal." A spirited discussion then took place among the forty other doctors. The president of the Medical Bureau, Dr. François Leuret, said: "This was a case of total idiocy and quadriplegic paralysis that had resisted many months of treatment." A Bordeaux doctor asked, "What brain does the child think with? A new brain, or the one partially destroyed by meningo-encephalitis?" Another doctor added, "However you answer that question, we have a case here that goes against medical principles we are certain about." Someone then raised the old question, "But could there be some unknown force or agent yet to be discovered, as radium was discovered, that will one day explain this boy's recovery?" Professor Lelong of Paris replied, "If anyone has come across a case of a postencephalitic idiot regaining normality as this child has, I vow never to sign another Lourdes medical report." None of the other forty doctors had even heard of a case in any way resembling Guy's recovery. Drs. F. Leuret and H. Bon in their book *Modern Miraculous Cures*[1] highlight that meeting and the dis-

[1] François Leuret and Henri Bon, *Modern Miraculous Cures: A Documented Account of Miracles and Medicine in the 20th Century*. Trans. A. T. Macqueen and John C. Barry (New York: Farrar, Strauss, and Cudahy, 1957).

cussion. The July 1951 bulletin of the Lourdes International Medical Association also carried a report of it. If some mysterious natural healing agent exists, why does it not occasionally work in the thousands of gatherings of sick people in hospitals and clinics around the globe? Why aren't there continual medical reports of other cases similar to these instantaneous healings reported at Lourdes and religious pilgrimage shrines?

There are many cases of the gradual regression of cancer, for example, often unexpected—but never instantaneous. Dr. E. Le Bec, a Paris surgeon who took over as president of the Lourdes Medical Bureau in 1917, wrote an important book, *Medical Proof of the Miraculous.*[2] He took up some famous cases of Lourdes cures, supplying details of X rays and reports from doctors and hospitals that proved beyond doubt the patients suffered from very physical and very threatening diseases, usually of some years' duration. He had personal involvement in some of the cures. He emphasized repeatedly: (1) The cures took place instantaneously. (2) Foreign matter such as cancer cells, cancer-caused toxins in the blood, lung lesions from TB, dead bone, lengthened varicose veins and so on disappeared from formerly diseased bodies without a trace. He challenged medical experts to present similar cases, from a nonprayer environment, where instantaneous healing has occurred. This instantaneous dimension is for Dr. Le Bec and the Medical Bureau a special characteristic in Lourdes miracles, demonstrating the presence and action of God. Were there mass healings at Lourdes, a doctor might wonder if there is not some unknown natural force in the atmosphere there. Le Bec pointed out that Lourdes miracles are relatively few and happen in a great variety of disparate places—some while bathing in the *piscines*, some during Mass or the Blessed

[2] E. Le Bec, *Medical Proof of the Miraculous*, English ed. (London: Harding and More, 1922).

Sacrament procession and some before the Grotto. Some have taken place six hundred miles and more away. People who were too sick or had no travel money simply prayed to Our Lady of Lourdes and were cured—instantaneously and completely.

In 1960, Belgian professor Louis Monden published a 368-page study on miracles that Cardinal Avery Dulles called a definitive classic on the subject.[3] Monden, a professor of religion and psychology at Louvain, detailed examples of modern miracles, above all at Lourdes, and noted they are essentially the same as those "discreet" miracles of Christ— definitely physical and sudden cures but always occurring in a spiritual atmosphere of faith and prayer, never flamboyant or for show, never self-aggrandizing, and essentially signs of God's love to the recipient and the witnesses. In the course of his lengthy and rigorous research, Monden hunted unsuccessfully for scientifically documented cures, in secular situations, similar to the instantaneous cures of physical diseases at Lourdes. He cited the disappointed attempt by the British Medical Association in 1954 to discover such authenticated cures.

Plenty of "authorities" have publicly denied the supernatural character of miracles at Lourdes, for example, *The Dictionary of Common Fallacies* in 1978.[4] It based its case on the secular dogma that all cures are merely psychological. It gave as one authority Dr. D. J. West and his book *Eleven Lourdes Miracles*. In my chapter on the cure of Marie Kerslake, I quoted Professor David Morrell of Saint Thomas' Hospital, London. The professor found West's attack on the Lourdes Medical Bureau investigation practices most unsatisfactory because it was unscientific.

[3] Louis Monden, *Signs and Wonders*, English ed. (New York: Desclée, 1996).
[4] Philip Ward, *A Dictionary of Common Fallacies* (England: Oleander Press, 1978).

A family on a Lourdes pilgrimage with paralyzed child.

West's book was published in 1957. A year later another doctor challenged its findings as unscientific. Dr. F. B. McCann, an Australian who topped his class in medicine in the finals at Sydney University Medical Faculty in 1922, had researched Lourdes miracles and sat in on discussions of cases brought before the Lourdes Medical Bureau. McCann was doubly disturbed by West's book: It received some favorable medical reviews in Britain and Australia. McCann suggested, in his 1958 book *Our Lady's Signature*, that West and the medical reviewers' opinions came from their "intense distaste for accepting anything supernatural". West had attacked Catholic "authorities" in general for credulity and Lourdes Medical Bureau President Dr. François Leuret in particular. He described Leuret as "one who would stop at nothing in his anxiety to find more and bigger miracles". According to McCann, West never attended a session under Dr. Leuret at the Medical Bureau—or even met the man. McCann describes Leuret as "one of the greatest and holiest characters I've met, down-to-earth, most calm and practical, one of the most difficult persons imaginable to convince that some particular recovery was of a miraculous nature". Far from "emotion and hysteria" at the Lourdes Medical Bureau, McCann's first impression was "the cold and unimpassioned hearing of an English court of an unexciting civil case". McCann detailed the thoroughness of doctors at the Lourdes Bureau—Catholic, Protestant, agnostic or total unbeliever— painstakingly examining X rays and laboratory reports and unceremoniously throwing out cases where the scientific data presented were not regarded as professional.

Ruth Cranston's experiences of Dr. Leuret and his Medical Bureau were similar to McCann's. She noted "openness and objectivity" as the hallmarks of these professionals. Among them were "dedicated scientists and seasoned veterans who return year after year". President Leuret, she wrote, is by any standard "a remarkable man: Legion of Honour, Croix de Guerre, Councillar of France, Professor of Medicine and also head of a large clinic in Bordeaux".

Dr. E. Le Bec, who had been a senior surgeon in Saint Joseph's Hospital, Paris, became president of the Medical Bureau in 1917. In his *Medical Proof of the Miraculous*, he devoted six pages to Yvonne Aumaitre, cured when she was one year and ten months old. What gave Le Bec special interest was his personal friendship with Yvonne's father, a doctor practicing in Nantes. Dr. Aumaitre left a signed three-page deposition at Lourdes after his daughter's cure and the following is taken from it.

Aumaitre wrote first of the shock he and his wife received when their third daughter, Yvonne, was born double-club-footed. This was in 1894, when medical science could do little to correct the situation. When the child was about fifteen months old, Dr. Aumaitre continued, his friend Dr. Boffin of Nantes operated—"a tenotomy of the tendo Achilles to endeavour redressing the position of the feet". Two jointed splints reaching to the thighs were attached to consolidate the position of feet and legs. Up till then, Aumaitre added, the knees deviated like the feet—"limbs and feet turning like those of a marionette".

The operation improved nothing. "The splints caused fatigue, the thighs and legs commenced to waste, so I took my daughter to Dr. Saquet for scientific massage. I had made for her boots with wooden soles, to the external side of which were fastened two iron rods to correct the position of the feet. In spite of this apparatus my child, even held firmly on both sides by her hands, could not stand for any length of time. She just dragged her feet along on the outer side, and it

A youth pilgrimage to Lourdes, during the day procession.

was impossible for her to make one step alone because her legs turned under her. She was in this condition when I took her straight to the Medical Bureau when we arrived in Lourdes, June 24, 1896. Later that day my wife and I went with great faith and emotion and prayed at the Grotto. Our tears fell silently."

The next day, having attended morning Mass and received Communion, they went to the *piscines*. The father stayed outside praying, while the mother and nurse went in to bathe the child, who cried and struggled in the water. No improvement then or later that afternoon, when the child was bathed again. Dr. Boissarie, president of the Medical Bureau, observed Yvonne walking in her wretched fashion, held up by her mother and nurse, her feeble legs continually doubling up under her. The parents persisted in prayer. There are quite a number of recorded Lourdes miracles that occurred after several pilgrimages or after a number of immersions in the baths or attendances at Mass or the Procession.

> On the morning of the 26th, after her third bath Yvonne began to walk by herself with a stability which could not have been more complete in the case of a normal child, making her first steps in a state of perfect equilibrium. The instantaneous nature of this result is of very special interest. We were all overcome by emotion. My father-in-law, formerly President of the Nantes Tribunal of Commerce was profoundly moved.
>
> That day Dr. Boissarie saw the child walk alone several times. On the next day, the morning of the 27th, at the Medical Bureau, Dr. Boissarie made her walk alone, having removed the iron supports. The wooden soles then acted only as ordinary soles. The knees as well as the legs had obtained their normal movements.
>
> To sum up, here is an infant with double club feet, with considerable wasting of the muscles of both legs, with the ligaments of the knees relaxed, operated on at 15 months

without result and in whom massage had produced practically no good, suddenly attaining her balance, walking with the same stability as other children of her own age, using and placing her feet quite normally. My medical confreres had said this child would not walk for several years. Suddenly, aged 22 months she walks as if she had always done so normally. I wish to emphasise this point: my child, not 2 years old instantaneously attained perfect equilibrium and was able to walk. This is very difficult to explain from a scientific point of view.

The will to walk, suggestion, faith healing, imagination are all absent. The various theories about suggestion all fail here. At this age a child cannot be hypnotised.... [This was written at the time Charcot was making his claims, without ever going to Lourdes, that all cures there were of "nervous" origin.]

In describing this case which touches me so closely I have desired to assume my share in thanking and making known Our Lady of Lourdes.

In presenting this signed statement by Dr. Aumaitre, Yvonne's father and his personal friend, Dr. E. Le Bec made several points in his book *Medical Proof of the Miraculous*. The first were medical: The surgical operation failed because of "the very atrophied condition of the muscles of the legs and thighs.... All that could be done surgically had been done." He admitted the possibility of more surgery at a later date and of the muscles eventually regenerating with the formation of new muscle fiber. But, he insisted, though this improvement was in the realm of medical possibility, a considerable length of time would have to be involved. The healing of Yvonne in a matter of hours (and her immediately walking) was "utterly beyond medical possibility".

Secondly, he noted that Dr. Boffin, who operated on Yvonne, and the numerous experts who had been consulted by the anxious father never contested the facts. Given the heated debates on Lourdes and spirited attacks by rationalists, those living in Nantes could easily have secured denials if the medical details given were false. In his book, which came out soon after the cure, Le Bec gave the doctors' names.

If there were just a few cases like these at Lourdes, it might be difficult to convince people that the cures were miraculous. However, such cases have occurred in great numbers, as Ruth Cranston pointed out, though they are few when compared with the numbers of sick who go there.

Cranston, daughter of a Methodist bishop, was an American writer who lived and died a Protestant. Her first stories were published when she was nineteen. Later on, her articles were published by periodicals such as *Harper's Magazine* and *Century*. From 1928 to 1938 she served on the World Conference on Religions at Geneva. She was also a member of the World Foundation of Churches. At the beginning of the 1930s she began to be especially interested in religious healing. Her book *World Faith*, an account of religions in the United Nations, was published in 1945. Then she discussed with a New York psychiatrist, Dr. Smiley Blanton, her plan to write a book on healing. He suggested she go to Lourdes— he had worked there with other doctors and was very impressed. Cranston researched Lourdes for three years and studied original Medical Bureau documents. (Her sister Ethel said she actually read "thousands" of Lourdes cases.) She brought out her 234-page book, *The Mystery of Lourdes*, in 1955. *Reader's Digest*, Chicago's *New World* and *McCall's Magazine* printed digest versions the same year. In 1988 an expanded edition was published as *The Miracle of Lourdes*.

Cranston quoted the president of the Lourdes Medical Bureau, Dr. François Leuret, as saying in August 1953, "We hold some 1,200 records and files of inexplicable cures, with orderly, systematic accounts, many including X rays and clinical reports, their doctors' diagnoses, etc. We have notes and materials on some 4,000 cases that are very probably complete and genuine cases, but without sufficient data to record them as cures. But the individuals and their families are undoubtedly enjoying the blessings of a genuine cure." Then Cranston gave her own personal opinion after three years of research in Lourdes, of reading much of the vast literature on the subject and of traveling around France to meet the cases she was writing about: "It is probably safe to say that during the 100 years of the Lourdes shrine [i.e., up to 1953] at least 10,000 have been healed there." The year she wrote that, two million pilgrims came to Lourdes. By 1984 the number was more than four million. When I was there in 1997, it was five and one-half million.

Dr. Patrick Theiller said in 1998, the year he was appointed president of the Medical Bureau: "Thinking people are coming on pilgrimage in greater numbers as a reaction to the consumer society and its indiscriminate rejection of principles that has led to materialism, to the unmarried living together, to increased divorce, to falling church attendance . . . and sermons that have preached relativism, watered down miracles and reduced God to the confines of secular science, psychology and psychoanalysis."

Lourdes miracles are proof to many seekers that God is real, that he loves us, that heaven is not an imaginary pie in the sky. Ruth Cranston said at the end of her book that Lourdes miracles were to her confirmation that the Scriptures are true. She saw in the cures at Lourdes a true reflection of Jesus of the Gospels, who healed bodies and spirits. "The road to Lourdes", she concluded, "is the road Back Home . . . Home to all homesick hearts . . . the Father's house, the beloved community: the end of the road when we pilgrims of all faiths and races come Home."

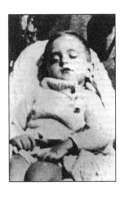

Chapter 9

A JEWISH TESTIMONY

And the Child Pascal

THE NAZI OCCUPATION of Poland, beginning on September 1, 1939, besides involving the butchering of millions of Poles, evokes grim images of Auschwitz and the genocide against the Jewish people. Franz Werfel was an Austrian Jew high up on the Nazi death list. In his twenties he fought on the German side in World War I. The horror he witnessed and the meaningless slaughter of young and talented friends left him disillusioned and tormented with doubt. He rediscovered the God of the Jewish faith in post–World War I years and soon established himself as a major poet, playwright and novelist. His antiwar writing incurred the enmity of Hitler's National Socialists. When they annexed his native Austria in 1938, he fled with his wife, Alma, to France. The Nazis stormed into France, and the couple fled south, hoping to get across the Spanish border and to the United States. But the borders were sealed, and they got only as far as Lourdes, where town dwellers gave them hospitality. It was June 1940.

"We hid for several weeks in Lourdes", he later wrote. "It was a time of great dread. The British radio announced that I had been murdered by the National Socialists. . . . It was also a time of great significance to me, for I became acquainted with the wondrous history of the girl Bernadette Soubirous and also with the wondrous facts concerning the healings of Lourdes. I vowed that if I escaped from this desperate situation and reached the saving shores of America I would put off all other tasks and sing, as best I could, the song of Bernadette."

He did escape to the United States, and in 1941 *The Song of Bernadette* burst onto American bookstands as a bestseller. It was quickly translated into seven languages. The movie studio 20th Century Fox soon turned the book into a box-office success under the same title. Jennifer Jones, who played Bernadette, won an Academy Award for her performance.

Many read Werfel's book or saw the movie as a powerful story of goodness, silhouetted sharply against the evil horizons of World War II's last battles. All Werfel's later writings had increasingly delineated a struggle of the good (God and redemption) against ever-present and virulent evil.

In the preface to *The Song of Bernadette*, Werfel wrote, "All the memorable happenings that constitute the substance of this book took place in the world of reality. Since their beginning dates back no longer than 80 years, there beats upon them the bright light of modern history and their truth has been confirmed by friend and foe and by unbiased observers. The story makes no changes in this body of truth."

Protestants (such as John Oxenham, Margaret Gray Blanton and, as previously mentioned, Ruth Cranston) have researched Lourdes and its miracles and found a corroboration of their belief in the Gospel miracles. Werfel, who lived and died a believing Jew, rejoiced that in writing of Lourdes he could "magnify the divine mystery and the holiness of man"

in an age that "has turned away with scorn and rage and
indifference from these ultimate values of our mortal lot". His
sensitivities as he wrote this book had been refined by hot-in-
pursuit Nazi executioners and by his solemn vow to the God
of Abraham and Moses. He certainly researched Bernadette
and Lourdes with great energy and skill. In 1997 the permanent chaplain at Lourdes, Fr. John Poole, O.M.I., spoke with
me about *The Song of Bernadette*. Werfel's book demonstrated
painstaking hands-on research, he said, of the major events
surrounding Bernadette and Lourdes. A practicing Jew—and
one who believed God saved him and his wife from the Nazis
and so made a vow to him to write the book as a testimony—
would hardly change the essential facts he had thoroughly
researched. What could be the possible motive of lying in
favor of a religious shrine not of his own faith? Many who
have written enthusiastically of Lourdes went there initially
without any faith in God or miracles.

Werfel wrote of the fierce, and at times bitter, struggle that
took place in Lourdes before Bernadette and the miraculous
spring were accepted. Having had personal encounters with
evil in World War I and later with Hitler's Nazis, Werfel
included long sections in his book on the perfidy of some
who tried to destroy Bernadette and her message from "the
Lady". He also gave a chilling description of what happened
at the beginning of the fourth apparition of the Lady. Bernadette spoke afterward of how a cacophony of harsh yells
assaulted her ears, "colliding with each other like the clamor
of a brawling crowd". Then a voice, more strident than the
others, dominated the chaotic screams with the menacing,
"belching order" to Bernadette and the Lady: "Get out of
here. . . . Get out of here." The Lady merely looked at the
nearby Gave River, from which the voices came. The shouting mob was reduced to silence—"Come to heel like a
daunted wolf", wrote Werfel, adding that the Lady's stern

look was of one who "still has to wage battles and vanquish enemies". Werfel had no hesitation in believing that Bernadette had met personalized wickedness, Satan and evil spirits, hellbent on destroying goodness, hope and love whenever they get a "hoofhold".

Werfel portrayed Bernadette as remarkably levelheaded and full of common sense. This is the Bernadette whom scores of fascinated historians and writers have described in their biographies. But this no-nonsense, self-possessed, disciplined-by-hardship Bernadette blanched and was deeply troubled when the Lady showed her the consequences of people "loving sin". Werfel's Lourdes is about a cosmic struggle, in which the stakes are for keeps. Carla Zawish, M.D., a fellow Austrian refugee, was in Lourdes at the same time as her old friends Werfel and his wife, Alma. She wrote: "I saw the deep emotion in Werfel [when he was in Lourdes]. . . . Never before had he been so profoundly shaken in all his being. A new world had opened before him, and he plunged into it with all his eagerness." Werfel's ideas about metaphysical good (the biblical God) and the mysterious pull of evil that is sin came into their sharpest focus in *The Song of Bernadette*. Bernadette's sufferings and struggles mirrored his own. And for Bernadette and himself, they ended in a song of praise for "the Redeemer", as Werfel came to see God.

The fifth chapter of Mark's Gospel tells a touching story of a twelve-year-old girl who is dying. Her desperate father, Jairus, is a synagogue official who risks the anger of the establishment by coming openly to Jesus. Jairus' love for his child is greater than any fear of personal loss. Mark says he "fell at Jesus' feet and pleaded, 'Come and lay your hands on her to save her life.'" As Jesus sets off with Jairus, servants arrive to say the child has just died. Jesus goes to the home anyhow, takes the small dead hand and says, "Talitha cumi" (Little girl, I say to you arise). She stands up cured, and Jesus tells her parents she will be hungry, so get her something to eat.

I remember in my early twenties reading this and other Gospel stories and agonizing: These stories, above all the one about the Resurrection, were the answers to my problems about the meaning of life and death, if they were true. But how can we possibly verify events two thousand years old! Maybe, in response to the bittersweetness of human life, kindly and imaginative people created the stories as they create fairy stories. Is Jairus' daughter any more real than Sleeping Beauty? At that time in my life, Lourdes miracles began to assume great importance. I read many books about them, searching for weak links in the evidence. I ended up concluding that miracles, essentially the same as the ones we read about in the Gospels—humanly inexplicable, supernatural events—are happening today at Lourdes. Lourdes brought me back to belief in the Jesus of the Gospels, Jesus who can suspend the laws of nature.

There are well-established cures of very young children at Lourdes. These cases have added importance as answers to people like the novelist Émile Zola, who puts Lourdes miracles down to autosuggestion or crowd-induced hysteria. Take, for instance, number forty-five in the list of canonical miracles.

François Pascal, born October 3, 1934, to a winegrower family in Beaucaire (about 37 miles west of Marseilles), was a healthy, energetic child until December 1937, when the three-year-old suddenly ran a temperature of 104 degrees. His eyes began to water, his arms and legs to stiffen and his sight to deteriorate. Local Dr. Darde, noting "flaccid paraplegia", suspected meningitis. The child was taken to the city of Avignon, where Dr. Lesbros performed a lumbar puncture, which confirmed the diagnosis of meningitis. By June the paralysis of arms and legs was total. Dr. Polger, an oculist in

Arles, gave the child's parents the grim verdict that he was now totally blind. There was absolutely no response to light. They sought other opinions, but no hospitals or clinics offered any more hope than Dr. Darde had given when he "discontinued treatment as pointless".

The annual Provence Lourdes pilgrimage was being organized for August. François' parents applied for a place and were told to furnish a medical certificate for their boy. Dr. Darde wrote out François' medical certificate on July 19. Dr. Roman, one of the pilgrimage doctors, read it as the group set out for Lourdes on August 23 and added: "The child is traveling lying down and quite blind."

Upon arrival François' mother carried the paralyzed child to the Lourdes Grotto "with strong faith" and begged the Virgin, "Heal him or let him die!" She took him to the baths, but the water produced no change. After being bathed the next day François was being carried across the esplanade by his mother. Suddenly he moved his hand, pointing to one of the three-wheeled carriages used to ferry the bedbound. "Maman, Maman," he said excitedly, "isn't it pretty?" The mother almost fainted. Then, in great excitement, she rushed the child back to his hospital bed. The child was excited, too, identifying objects in the ward and moving his limbs. Dr. Roman was sent for. Four days later they were back home, and François was taken straight down to Dr. Darde, who was stunned. The child walked and saw! Over the succeeding months Dr. Darde kept checking the child. By November 9 he was ready to write a signed statement, which the mother would take when she presented the child for examination in the Lourdes Medical Bureau the following August. The essentials of Dr. Darde's testimony are as follows:

> I, the undersigned, declare I had under my care from December 18, 1937, to June 14, 1938, François Pascal, age four. The child, seen in consultation with Drs. Julian of Tarascon, Barre

of Avignon, Dufoix Fils of Nîmes and Polge of Arles, had
been suffering from lymphocytic meningitis (analysis of Dr.
Lesbros of Avignon). At the end of July the patient was paralyzed in all four members. Visual acuity was nil. He did not
perceive even light and could not distinguish day from night.

Before the child was taken to Lourdes I was asked to
examine him (for a medical certificate). The condition I
recorded previously in June was exactly the same: paralysis of
four limbs, vision nil.

Returning from Lourdes (August 28) Madame Pascal
brought the child to me, leading him by the hand. He was
walking! I recorded the disappearance of paralysis and the
return of vision. From that date the improvement has been
maintained . . . medically speaking one cannot explain such a
result. (Signed, Dr. Darde, November 9, 1938.)

Nazi war clouds were gathering to the east; France began
feverish mobilization, and life was disrupted. The German
military smashed right through France, and the Lourdes Medical Bureau was closed down. It was not until after the war that
François Pascal's mother was able to bring him to Lourdes
with the medical dossiers from the local doctors. On October
2, 1946, in the large examination room of the Lourdes Medical Bureau, twelve doctors thoroughly probed François and
examined the medical papers his mother carried. They noted
he was now "a sturdy, tall and well-muscled boy who rides a
bicycle and attends a normal school". The 1938 illness, they
added, was definitely "organic" and not psychological. The
spinal fluid analysis and the lesions of the eyes were proof
positive it involved meninges of the spinal cord.

The report concluded, "When the development of the
illness left no hope of improvement, there was an abrupt
cessation of symptoms. The cure is confirmed by complete
recovery of vision, of the ability to walk and of all other
functions. . . . The cure is now of ten years' duration. There
is no medical explanation for the instantaneous disappearance

of the malady and its symptoms." Among the twelve doctors signing this initial statement was famous Dr. Auguste Vallet.

Auguste Vallet as a medical student at Bordeaux in 1898 heard Professor Pitres, dean of the medical faculty, propound, "If at any time you hear talk of so-called miraculous cures at Lourdes, realize this is nothing more than shameless exploitation of human stupidity." Vallet graduated, became a major in the French Army medical corps and was decorated in World War I. He was shocked, however, by the horrors modern warfare did to bodies and minds. He became more and more interested in Lourdes and the hope it gave to huge gatherings of the sick and afflicted. Lourdes moved him deeply and gave him hope. The endless lines of wounded and dying soldiers had scarred his optimism and almost demoralized him during wartime.

In 1927 he became president of the Lourdes Medical Bureau. He quickly set up its international branch with doctor-members from twenty-five nations. He called in outside specialists in 1928, 1933 and 1938 to analyze the waters that occasioned so many healings. Opponents of Lourdes, unable to deny many remarkable cures were occurring, suggested there were radioactive elements, electric resistivity or even penicillin in the water. The outside professors called in by Vallet could discover no such substances. The water was normal mountain-spring water.

Vallet was president of the Medical Bureau for twenty years, during which time he wrote several books on Lourdes miracles, lectured on them in many countries and coedited a magazine devoted to discussing the miracles scientifically. He said he was very happy to have become "our Lady's secretary".

Ruth Cranston, having researched the documentation on François Pascal's cure, went to Beaucaire in 1953 to interview him. It was then fifteen years since the cure. She found the nineteen-year-old youth in the bloom of health with perfect eyesight. He was an outdoors man, very much the son of his winegrower father, whose profession he intended to follow. François told her he went to Lourdes every year carrying the banner of the Provence pilgrimage and working as a stretcher bearer. He added that he was interviewed often by journalists and had his hands full answering letters from strangers inquiring about the miracle.

The child François Pascal, once unconscious and stricken with meningitis, several years after the cure.

Chapter 10

JEANNE FRETEL

"Poor Girl, She's Dead!"

THIS CURE WAS especially dramatic and has been discussed in many books about Lourdes. Jeanne Fretel was born May 27, 1914, in Sougeal, near the city of Rennes in Brittany—the Celtic region of France. The family was not well off, and Jeanne had to join the workforce while her peers were still at school. First she worked as a waitress and then became a nurses' aide in Rennes Central Hospital.

In January 1938, Jeanne began having stomach pains and was operated on for what was regarded as a simple appendectomy. After a normal postoperative stay, she was discharged from the hospital and went home to recuperate fully. This did not happen. Stomach pains returned, and in August she was readmitted to Rennes Central Hospital and given ultraviolet-ray treatment. There was temporary relief, but her stomach began to swell and become clammy to the touch. Dreaded tubercular peritonitis was diagnosed.

Though Jeanne had little money, she received special treatment because she was a member of the hospital staff. In January of 1939 Dr. Maruelle discovered a tuberculous cyst on one of her ovaries and operated to remove it. That same year a laparotomy—an incision the length of her stomach—was performed. Unfortunately, adhesions developed in her abdomen, and her stomach pains intensified. Ice treatment was tried but without success. Dr. Pellé, on the permanent staff of Rennes Central, tried another laparotomy in May 1941. Something went wrong, and Jeanne was left with a stercorale fistula—an unnatural passage allowing feces to seep out from the normal canal. It took four further operations—from December 1941 to September 1943—to close the fistula opening. The stomach remained swollen and hard, a classic example of tubercular peritonitis. By now the TB bacillae had spread to other parts of the body, so in January 1946 she was sent to a TB sanitarium at Pressac in Giroude. Three months later, with TB now in her jawbone, she was taken to the sanitarium La Benne-Ocean in Landes for three operations—leaving her with big holes in her jaw and only nine teeth.

By December of 1946, Jeanne weighed just ninety-seven pounds and felt completely exhausted. The staff decided there was no hope of recovery and packed her off to Pontehaillou, a hospice for the dying. She had now been bedridden for twelve months and was too weak to raise herself up in bed. "I knew I was dying", she said, recalling those days.

At this stage the new wonder drug for TB, streptomycin, came out on the French market. Dr. Pellé of Rennes Central decided it was worth a try and from April 1948 put Jeanne on the drug for forty-five days. She showed absolutely no improvement, so in June he discontinued treatment. Pellé's notes at that stage show Jeanne's temperature ranging from 104 degrees in the morning to 96.8 degrees in the evening, with her abdomen still swollen like a balloon and painful to the touch. She could manage only small quantities of liquid nourishment and had fits of coughing that brought up black blood. Copious pus appeared in her stools. She was receiving three to four shots of morphine daily. You can see these medical details in her file at Lourdes.

While the hospital chaplain was giving Jeanne the last rites on September 29, 1948 (for the third time), an acquaintance was booking her a place on the annual Dominican Fathers Rosary pilgrimage. Dr. Pellé would later write, in response to an official request from the Lourdes Medical Bureau investigating her cure, "In a state of fully developed tuberculosis peritonitis with meningeal symptoms superadded, the patient left from the Rennes Railway Station on October 4, 1948 . . . in a state of absolute exhaustion!" He felt quite cynical about the whole Lourdes exercise.

His cynicism seemed justified even before the pilgrim train had pulled out of Rennes Station. Jeanne had lapsed into unconsciousness due to the stress of being moved. Dr. Hylli, who was among the doctors accompanying the pilgrimage to Lourdes, gave her two morphine injections during the four-hundred-mile journey.

The train pulled into Lourdes the next day, October 5, 1948. The pilgrims lustily sang the famous Lourdes "Ave", though Jeanne heard, saw and knew nothing of what was happening. Nor was she conscious of being carried to the Grotto and the baths or of anything over the next several days.

Then came Friday, October 8! Two stretcher bearers carried the still-unconscious Jeanne to the Mass of the Sick at Saint Bernadette's altar. The priest noticed vomit running from Jeanne's mouth and black blood around her mouth and nostrils when he moved among the immobilized sick giving Communion and decided to pass her by. One of her stretcher bearers, feeling deep compassion for the pathetic woman, begged the priest to push a tiny fragment of the Host into her mouth. He did, and, said Jeanne, "I regained consciousness at that precise moment. 'Where am I?' I asked. 'At Lourdes', someone said. After Mass they took me to the Grotto on my stretcher. Some minutes elapsed. Then I had the sensation that someone was taking me under the arms to help me sit up! I found myself sitting and looked around to see who had helped but saw no one! . . . Next I had the feeling that the hands that had helped me sit now took my hands and put them on my stomach! I asked myself what could be happening. Was I cured, or was I just waking from a dream? I could perceive my stomach was now normal, and I was seized with an extraordinary hunger!"

Jeanne asked to see a doctor. The stretcher-bearers carried her to Dr. Gurgan, from Saint-Meen-la-Grand. She told him her stomach had returned to normal. The swelling and pain had disappeared, and she felt very hungry. Could she have something to eat? He examined her, found the stomach quite normal and said, yes, she could have something to eat. They went to the hospital kitchen and brought her purée and veal with three pieces of bread. She ate these without the slightest difficulty.

"I had been able to manage only liquids for the past two months, but now I enjoyed the kind of meal I had not eaten for ten years!" continued Jeanne. "I asked for more! They brought me as much again, and yet it wasn't enough! They gave me dessert, a dish of rice pudding." Then she got up by herself.

"I walked to the *piscines*. I had not walked for three years, but that afternoon I walked as well as I do now. I arrived there and took a shower-bath, standing and with no fatigue." She returned to the hospital, ate a substantial evening meal and went to bed—but awoke at 11 P.M., feeling hungry again! This sudden hunger after a cure of chronically ill people who have not eaten a real meal in months or years is a phenomenon you come across in many Lourdes miracles. There is a sudden return to normality and appetite in long-starved stomachs that, theoretically, should not be able to stand a big meal. And there follows an extraordinarily quick return over the next days and weeks to normal weight. (The hospital in Rennes remarked on this phenomenon when Jeanne returned there.)

She was told to go for a medical examination at the Lourdes Bureau on October 9, the day after her cure. Word had spread, and quite a group of doctors were waiting for her. Because she looked so emaciated, the hospital people insisted she go there on her stretcher. She was carried in and placed on a bed. Dr. Guyon of Nantes, acting as spokesman, welcomed her and, not knowing she had already been walking, suggested, "If you say you are cured, try to stand up and walk." Several doctors, seeing how frail she looked, moved to help her get up. She waved them away and got up unassisted. Dr. Guyon feared she might topple over—"I had no real legs anymore", she later commented—and he moved to steady her, but she waved him away. He nodded and walked briskly over to the scales. "I followed him, and though he walked quickly, I was just as fast to the scales", said Jeanne. A strong sense of confidence was surging through her.

The doctors examined her carefully. They had the pilgrimage doctors' report detailing her utter debility when leaving Rennes. They now found her stomach normal and no symptoms of her grave illness. Having jotted down careful observations for filing in the Medical Bureau, they told her to report back in a year's time with old and new medical reports from Rennes Central Hospital.

Jeanne Fretel left Lourdes after her remarkable experience and amazed her pilgrimage members during the train trip to Rennes. She was on her feet much of the time, moving around the carriages assisting and encouraging the sick who had not been healed. One nurse, worried by her sudden return to vitality and energy, "wanted to give me an injection to calm me. I refused and was able to rest well whenever I wanted. At home I took up my [hospital] work immediately. I have never taken even an aspirin since." (She said this to Ruth Cranston five years after the cure during an interview that took place at Lourdes after Jeanne had worked a long day as a volunteer caring for sick pilgrims. See *The Miracle of Lourdes*, pages 209–16.)

Jeanne went to the hospital upon arriving back at Rennes after her cure, stunning the staff. A young doctor sped to find Dr. Pellé and just blurted out, "Jeanne Fretel, Jeanne Fretel!" "Poor girl, she's dead", responded the older man. "Come and see", replied the messenger.

Dr. Pellé was thunderstruck when he saw her, so much so that he abruptly left the room for several minutes. When he returned, it was obvious he had been crying. He examined her thoroughly, finding no traces of her terminal disease.

Dr. Pellé was a declared agnostic, "hostile to religion", his professional acquaintances said. The Lourdes Medical Bureau files also note this, which gives his testimony a special nuance. He had treated Jeanne over a long period, and a mutual respect had grown between them. He was a conscientious doctor and over the following weeks and months checked and rechecked her health. He had written the report, requested by the pilgrimage organizers, quoted earlier in this chapter. After the cure, he scrupulously supplied medical charts, X rays and temperature charts to the Lourdes Medical Bureau—even though miracles had absolutely no place in his agnosticism. It showed the bigness of the man.

Jeanne returned to Lourdes just one year after her cure, bringing the latest medical reports from Dr. Pellé and the Rennes hospital. She was thoroughly examined at the

Jeanne Fretel back at Lourdes in 1998, fifty years after her cure,
with Father Jeannin, director of the Rosary pilgrimage.

Lourdes Medical Bureau by Drs. Guyon (of Nantes), Ricus-
sent (Montpellier), Taillejer (Beziers) and Delroise of her
own city, Rennes. Eighteen other doctors attended, all with
active voice in the examination. At its conclusion all twenty-
two doctors signed the following statement, dated October 5,
1949:

"Having regard to the striking history of sickness, the
importance of the documents in the case (numerous reports
and medical certificates, thirty temperature charts comprising
eighteen before the cure and twelve afterward, the number of
doctors who examined Jeanne Fretel at all stages of her illness
and on her journey to Lourdes, the careful work of daily
observation and the extraordinary abruptness of the phenom-
enal cure), it is impossible to put forward any medical explanation of the said cure. It must be regarded as beyond natural
laws." The report noted she was now 124.5 pounds and
measured 29 inches around the stomach. The unconscious

woman who had left Rennes for Lourdes just one year before was 97 pounds and 39 inches around the stomach.

The Lourdes Medical Bureau is managed wholly by doctors. A not insignificant number of doctors have found or refound their Christian faith through studying Lourdes miracles. They are conscious of an obligation to investigate so-called cures with absolute scientific strictness—lest science and the faith be brought into disrepute, not to mention their own reputations. To guarantee total objectivity, the bureau documentation on people claiming cures is open to anyone with a certificate to practice medicine. (Ruth Cranston quoted a statistic for 1953—fifteen hundred doctors signed the register that year and took part in examinations.)

Lourdes is situated in southwest France, close to the border with Spain. In 1947 the Medical Bureau, in order to make its work and files accessible to many more doctors, set up the Lourdes National Medical Committee in Paris. This committee of doctors reexamines all the documents and findings of cases judged medically inexplicable by the Lourdes Bureau. On March 12, 1950, the Paris committee, noting the continued health of Jeanne Fretel and the wealth of indisputable evidence, ruled that "all this leads us to conclude that this is a medically inexplicable cure". The Medical Bureau made a much quicker decision on Jeanne than is usual.

Many, if not most, bishops are prepared to leave the matter there. People who really want to know if miracles like those in the Gospels still happen can easily obtain books detailing conclusions of the Lourdes Bureau and Paris committee doctors. Some bishops, when a person from their diocese is cured, choose to go further and set up their own local canonical commission of doctors and theologians. If this commission passes the cure, the bishop rules that the miracle is a canonical cure and "a sign from God". (The New Testament does point out that evil spirits can cause "wonders".) On

November 20, 1950, Cardinal Archbishop Roques of Rennes, having accepted his canonical commission's report, declared Jeanne Fretel's cure a genuine miracle, a sign from God. It became number fifty-two of the canonically accepted miracles worked through Our Lady of Lourdes.[1]

Ruth Cranston interviewed many miracle cases while researching her classic book. She noted a very definite lack of attention seeking among them. None of them suggested they were healed because they were especially "good". A common trait was that they returned to Lourdes regularly as volunteer helpers of the sick. Cranston discovered that Jeanne returned every year for at least a week's volunteer work and back in Rennes was kept very busy answering letters from all over Europe and the world. The grateful woman said she had no right to refuse anyone a reply. She was often asked by Cardinal Roques and by doctors to tell her story at public meetings. Occasionally the cardinal asked her to talk with seekers who were not sure if God really existed or cared about us. The cardinal had discovered that her straightforward, uncomplicated approach helped many confused people. She even took part in a movie designed to help people's faith, though she did not enjoy that kind of "star" exposure.

MSM, France, put out an excellent video in March 1993. It contains lengthy footage taken at the Rosary pilgrimage to Lourdes, which is run by the Dominican Fathers during October, the month of the Rosary. Jeanne Fretel and the Dominican priest who gave her the Eucharist at the moment of her cure retell the story in this documentary. Both close to their eighties, they speak with great enthusiasm—"Age has not wearied them." *The Lourdes Magazine*, October 1998, carries a beautiful photo of Jeanne, again at the Rosary pilgrimage, fifty years after her cure. Besides Cranston, many

---

[1] Théodore Mangiapan, *Lourdes: Miraculous Cures*, 3rd ed. (Lourdes Medical Bureau, 1997).

others have written about the Jeanne Fretel story, among them Joseph Deery in *Our Lady of Lourdes*[2] and Michel de Saint-Pierre in *Bernadette and Lourdes*.[3] The latter has photos of the Rennes hospital temperature charts and of the signatures of the doctors of the Lourdes Medical Bureau who passed this cure.

[2] John Deery, *Our Lady of Lourdes* (Westminster, Md.: Newman Press, 1958).
[3] Michel de Saint-Pierre, *Bernadette and Lourdes* (New York: Farrar, Straus and Young, 1954).

Chapter 11

PIERRE DE RUDDER

Lourdes' Most-Discussed Miracle

MAYBE THERE WAS some unknown but natural force in the water or even in the atmosphere around the Lourdes mountains that caused the extraordinary healing, some said. Like, for instance, those powerful forces that lay unknown for years in uranium—or the radium and polonium that Marie and Pierre Curie discovered in pitchblende in 1898, ushering in the era of X-ray therapy. This seems an obvious possibility in Lourdes cures, which is why so many who have studied the matter have spent much time on the case of Pierre de Rudder, who visited a Lourdes shrine in Belgium.

De Rudder was employed by Viscount du Bus de Gisignies, who had an estate about halfway between Bruges and Ostend in West Flanders, Belgium. On February 16, 1867, forty-five-year-old Pierre was helping two woodcutters shift a large tree they had just felled. The trunk suddenly moved, crushing Pierre's left leg, smashing both tibia and fibula below

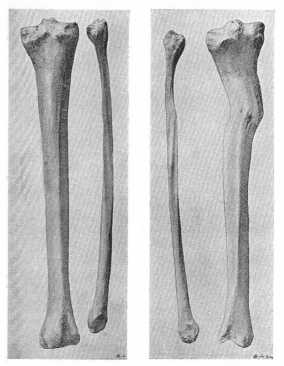

The tibia and fibula bones of Pierre de Rudder's legs after autopsy.
The mark of the fracture is visible on the left leg (right panel).

the kneebone. Dr. Affenear of nearby Oudenbourg set the
bones and bound the leg in starched bandages. The patient
suffered intensely, and when the doctor removed the bandages some weeks later, he was shocked to find "the broken
ends of the bones swimming in pus. They had not even
begun to knit." The doctor removed a bone fragment and
called in three other doctors. The verdict: Amputation was
the only option. Pierre adamantly refused and spent the next
painful year in bed. There was no sign of knitting, and the
ends of the bones became necrosed (dead) and blackened.

Bandages on the festering wound had to be changed three times a day.

The viscount allowed Pierre, whom he liked and admired, to live rent free on the estate and gave him a quite-small pension. He had a specialist, Dr. van Hoestenberghe of Stahille, see the cripple late in December 1874. In his report, the doctor noted that the ends of the bones could be seen in the open wound, with about an inch separating them. He added this gruesome detail: "He had endured this break for eight years. The lower part of the leg could be turned in any direction. The heel could be lifted so as practically to fold the leg in half. The foot could be twisted until the heel was in front and the toes at the back." He said amputation was the only possible course. Pierre again refused. The viscount consulted Dr. Verrist of Bruges some weeks later. When the patient again refused an amputation, these two doctors told the viscount they were giving up the case.

Pierre asked his employer, who had told him he would willingly pay for the amputation and all medical expenses, if he would pay for a trip to the shrine of Our Lady of Lourdes at Oostacker, a considerable distance to the east on the road to Ghent. The viscount told him not to be ridiculous. He would waste no money on superstition!

The viscount died, and in early April 1875 Pierre went to the castle again to ask the viscount's son and successor to get him to Oostacker. The new viscount's fiancée and his cousin happened to be visiting and requested to see this "turning leg" they had heard about. Everyone was shocked when the bandages were removed. The young viscount agreed to the impoverished Pierre's request, providing money for the train and bus trip.

On April 6, the eve of the pilgrim journey, three neighbors called in on Pierre—two van Hoorens and Marie Wittizache. They observed the wound being dressed and three weeks later signed a statement about the festering wound and "the bones separated by about an inch in the swinging left lower leg".

On the morning of April 7, when Pierre de Rudder was about to set out for the train station, Pierre Blomme, the gatekeeper, tried hard to talk him out of the painful "and useless" journey. It was to no avail. "Others have been cured at Oostacker, so why not I?" replied de Rudder doggedly. He was receiving little support for his pilgrimage. However, Blomme let him and his family rest in the gatehouse, helped them to the station and lifted him into the train—aided by a station hand and the local shoemaker, Jean Duclas. The latter later testified about the swinging leg and the sodden and foul-smelling bandages.

Pierre and his wife changed to a bus at Ghent bound for the shrine at Oostacker, where the burly bus driver lifted him to the ground. He couldn't believe it when he saw Pierre's left leg "swinging". With the insensitivity that sometimes accompanies robust health and size, he said to people at the bus stop, "Hey, look! Here's a man whose leg is coming off." His bouncing laugh stopped when he got into the bus and saw the blood and pus on his floor. He shouted angrily. All this would go into the testimony he gave later.

Pierre was tiring badly by now. Though the shrine was close by and his wife supported him, he hobbled very slowly and fell exhausted onto a seat in front of the shrine. His wife brought him a cup of water. Another pilgrim accidentally bumped his leg, setting it swinging and causing intense pain. In great distress Pierre turned his gaze to the face of the Virgin's statue, "asking pardon for my sins and begging Our Lady of Lourdes for the grace to be able to earn a livelihood for my wife and children". Then suddenly he felt a strange sensation and was upset, shaken, agitated. Forgetting his crutches, inseparable companions for the last eight years, he rose, walked through the rows of pilgrims and knelt in front

Pierre de Rudder—his legs after his cure.

of the statue of Mary. Then, astonished to find himself kneeling, he cried, "I am on my knees! O my God!" Getting to his feet he walked again, needing no help. His wife cried out, "What are you doing?" Then like a bolt came the realization, and she fainted.

Pilgrims crowded around the bemused Pierre and his wife. He was taken to a nearby chateau. The left leg seemed as sound as the right. The swellings had disappeared, and both legs were the same length again. Having submitted himself to this examination, Pierre went back to the shrine to thank the Virgin. Then he and his wife set off for home.

At the gatehouse Blomme momentarily lost his power of speech. Then he said, "You did well not to listen to me!" When Pierre walked into his home, his fifteen-year-old daughter, Silvie, fell into his arms, sobbing. The neighbors, who had thought it all so sad the night before, raced in when they heard the news. Someone wired the viscount, who was in Brussels. He said to his mother and fiancée, "I've never believed in miracles. If this report is true, I'll become a believer!" Within days neighbors and others who had known the cripple drew up a statement. The viscount was among the signatories. Of the two thousand parishioners, fifteen hundred responded to the parish priest's call for a novena of thanksgiving. Dr. Affenear, who had set the leg in the first place and felt some guilt, came from Audenbourg on hearing the rumor. He cried openly when he examined the leg and said to Pierre, "The Blessed Virgin has done what our remedies failed to do."

He notified Dr. Hoestenberghe, the specialist in Stahille. The doctor prided himself on being "a freethinker and unbeliever" and stated categorically that Pierre de Rudder could not be walking. When pressed, he decided to go to see his old patient. When he turned up, Pierre was hoeing his front garden, and, noticing Dr. Hoestenberghe's quizzical, doubting look, he laughed and began jumping up and down on both feet! The thunderstruck doctor examined both legs, finding them exactly the same length. The muscles of the left leg, despite eight years of wasting, were firm and strong! Seventeen years later Dr. Hoestenberghe read in the papers that Émile Zola, the French novelist and freethinker, was going to visit and study Lourdes and write a book about it. (That book, which came out in 1894, will be treated in a subsequent chapter.) Dr. Hoestenberghe wrote a quite extraordinary letter to the Lourdes Medical Bureau, asking them to show it to Zola if possible. The letter spoke of the

Pierre de Rudder miracle and how it set the freethinking doctor on a new and sometimes winding journey. "I still doubted sometimes, but I studied the Christian religion and prayed", wrote the doctor. "Now, I can affirm on my honor that I believe absolutely and that with belief I have found happiness, and an inner peace, which I had never known before."

Testimonies were signed by people who had seen Pierre before and after his instantaneous cure on April 7, 1875, within weeks of the event. Newspapers took up the story, and it became a cause célèbre across Belgium and much of Europe. In 1893 a Frenchman, Dr. Royer, came to Belgium while Pierre was still alive and vigorous to reexamine him and the witnesses. As the Frenchman did not speak Flemish, he engaged a translator, the latter being an avowed unbeliever in the supernatural. Dr. Royer thought this unbelief would sharpen the translator's thoroughness. The evidence, which resulted in the same conclusions as the original investigations, was so strong that the translator, in a personal addendum to the report, stated that his antireligious views were shaken. The only explanation for the cure must be a supernatural one!

Pierre de Rudder died of pneumonia on March 22, 1898, twenty-three years after the cure. Later on, the freethinker-turned-believer, Dr. Hoestenberghe, asked the family's permission to exhume the body and amputate the legs. They agreed to this extraordinary request, knowing Pierre's vigorous testimonies to the Virgin's goodness during the heated controversies following the cure. The original leg bones are still kept in the University of Louvain. Exact copper reproductions were made and sent to the Lourdes Medical Bureau. You can see them there today.

Dr. E. Le Bec's *Medical Proof of the Miraculous* discussed the de Rudder case—as most Lourdes books did at that time. He pointed out the two bones were separated by more than one inch. Furthermore, the ends had necrosed (died) and were black before the "instantaneous joining". That meant, he stated, nearly two inches of bone were instantaneously added to the tibia and fibula of the left leg. The weight of phosphate of lime required for this was five grams. However there are only 1.6 grams in a person's bloodstream. Both the instantaneous nature of the cure and the amount of phosphate of lime suddenly appearing cannot be explained medically. Medical literature has no such examples.

Again, Le Bec argued, muscles unused for eight years would atrophy. Tendons would contract adhesions in their sheaths. From a medical point of view, to get Pierre de Rudder walking more or less normally again (abstracting from the missing bone) would necessitate a lengthy period of massage, hydrotherapy and electricity. In a matter of seconds the almost dead-leg Pierre was walking briskly without any sign of abnormal gait. He immediately took up farm work on his return home and continued unhindered by any leg difficulty for another twenty-three years. On the very day after his cure his doctor, Affenear, verified a complete cure.

Chapter 12

GABRIEL GARGAM

The Corpse That Walked

IN MY OWN STRUGGLE to believe in Christ and the Church and even in "the good God" when I was in my early twenties, I was especially impressed by a Lourdes miracle cure written up at length in a number of books, including *The Hand of God*, by Martin Scott, S.J.,[1] and *After Bernadette*, by Don Sharkey.[2] I still have the notes I made at the time, a half century ago!

Gabriel Gargam, a postal clerk in his thirties, was sorting mail on the Bordeaux-to-Paris express, December 17, 1899. About midnight it slowed to a halt around a sloping bend near Angoulême. Then there was a horrific crash as another train, traveling at least fifty milers per hour, smashed into it.

[1] Martin J. Scott, *The Hand of God: A Theology for the People* (New York: P. J. Kenedy and Sons, 1918).
[2] Don Sharkey, *After Bernadette* (Milwaukee: Bruce Publishing Company, 1945).

A fellow mail sorter was killed instantly. Gabriel Gargam was found at 7 A.M. the next morning lying unconscious in the thick snow. They rushed him to Angoulême City Hospital, where doctors worked desperately to save his life. Twenty months later he was still in that hospital, paralyzed from the waist down, weighing only seventy-seven pounds, unable to eat. He could take nourishment only with difficulty through an esophageal tube. Gangrene was invading his sensationless feet.

The family had rejected the Orleans Railroad offer of an annual pension of 3,000 francs a year. In the ensuing court case, Dr. Decrassac, head of the Angoulême Hospital, issued a detailed medical statement: Gabriel Gargam was a cripple for life and a physical wreck, unable to do anything, requiring constant nursing care—"hardly susceptible of improvement; more likely to terminate fatally". The court ordered the company to pay Gargam the then-huge sum of 660,000 francs, plus 6,000 francs yearly. Orleans Railroad went to the appellate court but lost. The original damages were upheld.

Gabriel's condition worsened, and he was told he must have a spinal operation or he would die. He refused and asked his family to take him home, which they did.

Gabriel had not been to church for eight years and declared he was an unbeliever. His mother doubled her prayers for this son whom the doctors said would soon be dead. She begged him to let her take him to Lourdes. Soon, in the last week of August, the French national pilgrimage would take place. He refused point-blank. She persisted. His father urged him, too. The hospital contacted him again, begging him to have the operation before it was too late. Maybe just to shut them all up, Gabriel agreed to go to Lourdes.

They got him to the station on a stretcher, where he fainted. The authorities urged his mother to take him home. She refused. When Gabriel awoke, a priest gave him the sacrament of reconciliation and a tiny piece of Holy Communion. Gabriel showed little faith.

The train pulled into Lourdes at 7 A.M., August 20, 1901. Gabriel was sick and in pain and refrained from demanding an end to the whole business only for his devoted mother's sake. She, a nurse and a family friend walked beside him as stretcher bearers carried him to the Grotto, where Mass was said and he received a tiny particle of Host. Suddenly, he said, he knew God was real and loving. He began to pray with all his heart, laid his life at our Lady's feet and was filled with happiness. Said Gabriel, "It was the greatest moment of my life."

At 2 P.M. he was carried to the baths. His skeletal frame was lowered into the cold spring water, and the shock seemed too great. Gabriel lost consciousness. Outside, the distraught mother felt his lifeless face. It was cold. "He's gone", she murmured. Quite some time had elapsed when the sorrowing group, accompanied by the *brancardiers* carrying Gabriel's stretcher, headed back to the hospital. On the way they came across the procession of the Blessed Sacrament and stopped. The bishop carrying the monstrance saw them, paused and blessed Gabriel, who was lying with a cloth over his apparently lifeless face.

Gabriel stirred and gripped the sides of the stretcher with hands so thin they looked like claws. He struggled to rise. "Help me, I can walk, I feel I can walk." His mother sobbed out, "Hear him, Blessed Virgin, hear him! He has not spoken out loud for twenty months!" People helped him to his feet, and he took his first steps. The colorless face, the wasted body and the long nightshirt that looked like a shroud made him appear like a corpse walking. A crowd from the procession surged around him excitedly. He was taken back to the hospital and his mother and nurse were stunned to see another phenomenon often witnessed at Lourdes—a person

Dr. Boissarie.

who has not eaten normally for a long time has a hearty meal with no ill consequences. Gabriel calmly polished off soup, oysters, chicken and a bunch of grapes! After he had eaten, streams of visitors came, and he patiently told and retold his story.

When Gabriel reported to the Medical Bureau the next morning, he wore a new suit he had just bought and walked without difficulty. The word had got around. More than sixty doctors and a number of journalists were there—some remembered the newspaper reports of the court case that pitted the skeleton of a man dying in Angoulême Hospital against an apparently unfeeling, avaricious railroad company. People had cheered when the railroad lost both cases.

Dr. Boissarie was there when Gabriel reported to the doctors. Dr. Boissarie was to work at Lourdes for thirty years, was second president of the Medical Bureau and published

The Medical History of Lourdes in 1901—in which he challenged Émile Zola and Professor Jean Charcot (who claimed Lourdes "miracles" were through autosuggestion) to explain Gabriel Gargam's cure.

Dr. Boissarie describes Gabriel's eerie appearance. He "looked like a specter". There were sixty-three doctors present for the thorough medical examination. Among other phenomena Dr. Boissarie commented on was the absence of leg muscles after twenty months of total paralysis of both legs and no solid food. "Gentlemen," Dr. Boissarie remarked, "we must first certify that from a medical point of view M. Gargam cannot walk because he has no muscles." Gabriel again stood up and walked in front of them without difficulty. One doctor argued over the precise medical description of what was healed. Another replied, "What's the point of naming the malady. . . . The organism was destroyed. Now, without a period of convalescence, the man stands erect!" The doctors' examination took two hours. That was August 21, 1901.

Gabriel returned home. People had read about his cure in the papers and waited at stations along the way to see him. For the next fifty years he went annually to Lourdes, doing the heavy lifting work of a stretcher bearer. When the writer Georges Bartrim was collecting material for his book on Lourdes, he sent an urgent message. He was in Lourdes, had little time and wished to interview Gabriel that morning. A fellow *brancardier* found Gabriel working in the baths. Gabriel replied he was too busy with the sick to meet then. Bartrim would have to wait until evening—the sick have first priority. They are the important ones at Lourdes.

Gabriel married a woman who shared his faith and love for Lourdes. She accompanied him each year when he took a vacation from his business to go on pilgrimage. He served as a *brancardier* and she as a "handmaid", one of the volunteer women who wait on sick pilgrims. Gabriel Gargam went to Lourdes on pilgrimage for the last time in August 1952, fifty-one years after his miracle. He died the next March, in his eighties. I saw a touching photo of him taken in 1951 at Lourdes. He was walking in the Blessed Sacrament procession, quite erect despite his eighty-plus years, wearing the leather shoulder straps that are the badge of a *brancardier*. On his face was the serenity of a man who had met great tragedy and within it met God—and spent the next half century in compassionate service to the sick.

Chapter 13

ÉMILE ZOLA

"Frightful Pain"

É MILE ZOLA, at the age of seven, was stunned by the sudden death of his exuberant civil-engineer father, in 1847. From then until he was in his early twenties, he eked out a painful and often precarious existence with his widowed mother, imbibing her bitterness toward the establishment. Mother and child were in economic distress, she fiercely believed, because civic authorities were cheating them out of the pension that should have come after the death of her husband. When Émile Zola eventually became a successful journalist, critic and novelist, he took revenge by trenchant attacks on the establishment. This assuaged his hurt, and he was happy to discover that notoriety in newsprint increased sales of his novels. For him the Church was very much part of the establishment. His strong anti-Catholicism is very evident in his novels *Lourdes* (1894) and *Rome* (1896).

To understand his bias against Lourdes, I carefully read *Zola: A Life*, which Frederick Brown brought out in 1995—backed by the Guggenheim Foundation.[1] Zola wrote of Lourdes as a place where "money flows in torrents"—especially for the clergy—and "obsessively sung hymns . . . induce a state of nervous exaltation" leading to "apparently" mystical effects. The "religious magic . . . and hocus-pocus . . . do wonders for people with nervous dispositions but for poor tuberculous sufferers immersed (in the baths) . . . spell certain, often instant death". These claims astounded Dr. Boissarie, head of the Lourdes Medical Bureau. He challenged Zola to substantiate them. Zola declined.

Zola said he was confident he had "laid bare all the secret dramas . . . and unveiled all the mysteries of Lourdes". The seer Bernadette Soubirous, whose claims of eighteen apparitions from heaven began the Lourdes phenomenon, was dismissed by Zola as "an emotionally distraught girl", not only "a hysteric but also an idiot".

I sympathize with Zola's attack on the Church as part of the French establishment that did little to help the Zolas, and so many like them, living in grinding poverty. However, I find it hard to discover any honesty in his portrayal of Bernadette. He put fictitious statements about her into the mouths of some obscure and docile (he thought) Lourdes folk. When these statements came out in print, the latter quickly emerged from obscurity and hotly denied having said these things about Bernadette. Zola had either made no attempt to investigate Bernadette's character or had deliberately falsified what he discovered.

Zola spent thirteen days in Lourdes, from August 19 till September 1, 1892. That was a mere twenty-six years after twenty-two-year-old Bernadette left Lourdes to join the Nevers Convent. Most of her contemporaries and many of

[1] Frederick Brown, *Zola: A Life* (Farrar, Strauss and Giroux, 1995).

the original witnesses were still alive in 1892 and readily giving interviews about the now-famous Bernadette, dead only thirteen years. There was plenty of careful documentation on Bernadette, which Zola could have obtained easily. There was *La Grotte de Lourdes*, published in 1874 by Dr. Dozous, the Lourdes resident doctor who witnessed the apparitions and examined Bernadette very carefully with special regard to her mental health. Then there was *L'Apparition de la Grotte de Lourdes*, published in 1862 by Canon Fourcade, secretary of the Lourdes Investigation Commission set up by Bishop Laurence. The commission took almost four years of painstaking research before printing its conclusions.

Émile Zola.

In 1869 the barrister Henri Lasserre published *Notre-Dame de Lourdes*, having been given free access to the voluminous archives in Bishop Laurence's diocesan office. There were also the exhaustive notes taken by the investigator Leonard Cros, S.J., later published in book form and recognized as authoritative. Bernadette was scrutinized, analyzed and psychoanalyzed as few people have been. Zola either made no attempt to research the available material for his lengthy book, which was irresponsible, or deliberately changed the evidence, which would be worse.

Bernadette and the eighteen apparitions were an embarrassment to the civic authorities in 1858, a period in French history when scientism and rationalism held sway. Lourdes Chief of Police Jacomet, Imperial Prosecutor Dutour and Baron Massy, head of the whole geographical area, tried strenuously and repeatedly to force Bernadette into admitting a hoax. They eventually sent three doctors to "discover" her mental sickness. One of the three, Dr. J. B. Balencie, later publicly confessed to the loaded "investigation".

I have right here in front of me thirty-nine books on Bernadette. One of the most impressive for demolishing Zola's sham Bernadette is *We Saw Her*, by the Englishman B. G. Sandhurst. This ex-army man who fought in French trenches in World War I and North African deserts in World War II marshaled the evidence like a capable military officer preparing for a counterattack. Sandhurst was responding to fierce attacks by people like Zola, who fought under the flag of rationalism, which holds, as one of its principles, that miracles do not and cannot happen. Therefore Bernadette, Lourdes and the Bible must be demolished as dangerous frauds.

Sandhurst made it his business to collate a mass of written material about Bernadette and to meet direct witnesses still living—the daughter-in-law of key witness Nicolau the

Bernadette Soubirous soon after the apparitions.

miller, for instance. These witnesses, whom he quoted extensively, are the "We" of the book's title. Here they are:

1. Bernadette's parents, siblings and direct relations.

2. Police Chief Jacomet, Prosecutor Dutour and Prefect
Baron Massy. The official documents they left show the latter
did their best to discredit the apparitions by atempting to
prove that Bernadette was mentally sick or a fake.

3. Parish priest Peyramale, who initially decided the apparitions were not genuine, kept totally away from the site and
ordered his three curates to do likewise. When he eventually
came to accept the evidence, he defended Bernadette against
the civil authorities, personally preventing them from sending

her away to a distant mental hospital. He doubted her truth-fulness at first but always knew she was perfectly sane.

4. Bishop B.-S. Laurence initially followed the parish priest's hostile attitude. The Catholic Church was under attack in 1858 France, and the bishop envisaged the damaging public-ity if he in any way encouraged events that were later proven fraudulent. When the parish priest and on-the-spot authori-ties such as Dr. Dozous changed their minds on Bernadette's reliability and reported many good fruits and the seemingly incontestable physical healings, the bishop set up an official commission to investigate Bernadette and the whole matter vigorously. The commission was in no hurry, very conscious of the ridicule already heaped on Bernadette and Lourdes by rationalist journalists in the prefecture and in Paris. The commission spent close to four years investigating Bernadette, witnesses and the reported miracles before publicly endorsing Bernadette—and finding seven of the cures as beyond medi-cal explanation.

5. Also prominent among "We" was J.-B. Estrade, a rank-ing tax official who wrote articles for the Lourdes newspaper, the weekly *Lavedan*. He dismissed the story as preposterous when he heard it secondhand. He went to the seventh appa-rition, February 23, only because his sister Emmanuélite badgered him into chaperoning herself and her lady friends, who would not walk unaccompanied through dark streets to attend the predawn rendezvous of Bernadette at the Grotto. Estrade was later present when Police Chief Jacomet grilled an uncringing Bernadette, threatening jail if she did not stop the nonsense. The year before, he had jailed her father on suspicion of an unsolved crime. Estrade was impressed by Bernadette's undemonstrative but confident composure un-der the policeman's hostile cross-examination—as he was by the ecstatic transfiguration of this uneducated, poor girl dur-ing the apparitions. Estrade's book, *Les Apparitions*, paints a

strong, commonsense, alert Bernadette, the very antithesis of Zola's "emotionally distraught . . . hysteric idiot".

6. Sandhurst also gave the lengthy testimony of M. Clarens, teacher (and later headmaster) of the Lourdes Primary School in 1858. He had been a complete sceptic and decided to attend an apparition so that he could expose the whole dangerous affair as a hoax. He went on Saturday, February 27, and witnessed the tenth apparition. An experienced school-teacher, he was confident of his shrewdness in summing up children and their little ploys and deceits. He wrote, "I flattered myself I would be able to pick holes in her story and persuade her not to return to the Grotto." He called on Bernadette for a long conversation that left his "theories turned upside down". Clarens eventually became a believer, and, in the midst of the hostility of the civil authorities toward Bernadette, put his job on the line by writing a report defending her to Prefect Baron Massy. The schoolmaster became her public ally. He published a detailed report about her and the apparitions in 1861.

7. Sandhurst collected the testimonies of thirty-six other Lourdes dwellers who knew Bernadette. The picture that emerged of her is very clear. Bernadette was remarkably self-possessed, quick-witted (sometimes too much so for her own good!), transparently honest and equipped with peasant common sense, demonstrating no exaggerated emotionalism.

Zola, who on one occasion had dismissed the common people as "imbeciles", had dismissed Catholicism as dying "occultism", without a future. In 1864 he had written of "the depopulated heaven" and boasted how the rationalists (among whom he saw himself as a leader) had bequeathed to coming generations "a sky purged of ghosts". He was staggered at the vigor and swiftness of public Catholic challenges to his book *Lourdes*.

The much-published writer Frances Parkinson Keyes is

one of the many biographers of Bernadette who went to Lourdes to research the original documents in French. Like Sandhurst, she also spoke with surviving witnesses, such as Bernadette's sister-in-law. In the preface of her *Bernadette of Lourdes*, Keyes confessed that she fell under the spell of "the splendor of spirit" of this Cinderella from the slums who became a spiritual princess.[2] Bernadette, she wrote, was "intelligent, composed and full of fortitude; hysteria and cowardice were alien to her nature and fine mentality.... She had the courage of her convictions and steadfastly clung to them in the face of all opposition." Keyes highlighted the strenuous efforts of the municipal authorities to force Bernadette to recant and put a stop to her "dangerous" experiences at the Grotto of Massabielle. Keyes was delighted to discover Bernadette never lost her fine sense of humor and ability for playful mimicking. Even when she was dying in the convent infirmary, she delighted fellow nun patients by imitating the grave manner of their doctor.

Why did Zola portray Bernadette as an unrecognizable caricature? Why did he insist, shrilly, that the only cures at Lourdes were psychological, easily explicable by medical experts? He certainly had reason to despise the hypocrisy of the establishment, of which the Church was a part. And without doubt, a public pose as a churchman or a practicing Christian increases the ugliness of any hypocrisy. He attacked such people with zest and relish, and good for him.

Zola was a man of energy and creativity, and of great courage. Almost single-handedly he defeated the state and won freedom for Alfred Dreyfus, a falsely imprisoned Jew, thereby exposing the ugliness of anti-Semitism. Did he do this, however, purely from altruistic motives or also because he enjoyed his attacks on establishment figures, which brought him publicity and increased the sale of his books?

[2] Frances Parkinson Keyes, *Bernadette of Lourdes* (New York: Messner, 1947).

Perhaps a major reason for Zola's hatred of Christianity was his personal immorality, which, together with his novels—laced with marital infidelities, incest and other evils—would hardly make him feel comfortable with the stand taken by Jesus of Nazareth. I think we have many people like Zola today, people who know and use the destructive power of the media, very often leading the nondiscerning on wild goose chases and worse.

Zola, a fiercely proud man, did not enjoy criticism from anyone—you see this in the way he turned on critics of some of his plays, even notably unsuccessful plays. Jesus warned of the danger of riches that easily lead to that arrogance which, he said, makes entry into the Kingdom of God very difficult. Riches are not restricted to money. Successful writers, artists and intellectuals possess riches that can be very seductive, that can harden the heart against God's will manifested in the intimacy of conscience.

When Zola's mother, Emilie, died in 1880, the forty-year-old Zola felt constrained to have her buried from a parish church. Later he wrote to Henry Céard of the "frightful pain" the religious ceremony gave him. I believe his efforts to destroy the credibility of Bernadette and Lourdes were efforts to rid himself of the "frightful pain" that the ethical teaching of the Bible gave him—a teaching strongly reiterated in the life of Bernadette Soubirous and in the messages about sin and repentance given her by the Lady during the apparitions.

The first apparition at Lourdes, February 11, 1858.

Chapter 14

EXPOSING A ZOLA FICTION

Three People of Straw

HITLER'S MINISTER OF public enlightenment and propaganda, Joseph Goebbels, had gained a doctorate of philosophy from Heidelberg University. His learning proved no obstacle to his doctoring the truth! He became a master of spin doctoring and disinformation and knew even a lie sticks in people's minds if repeated often enough. I've come across much disinformation about Lourdes, and I return to Zola's book *Lourdes*, his subsequent reactions to criticism and a recent biography of Zola as classical examples of this.

Zola knew the power of the media and courted it. He airily announced to journalists from *Le Figaro* and *Gil Blas* that he was going to uncover "the facts" about Lourdes. He added that Catholics need have no fears: He would write his book "without any malevolent intention". He stayed in Lourdes from August 19 to September 1, 1892. Dr. Boissarie, head of the Medical Bureau, opened all doors for Zola and invited him to attend doctors' sessions examining people

Clementine Trouvé—Sophie Couteau in Zola's Lourdes.

claiming cures, which Zola did on two occasions, August 20 and 21. Zola had previously told journalists that Lourdes could cure only people with "nervous afflictions". Dr. Boissarie made a point of presenting patients healed of very physical diseases. I will discuss three of these physical or "organic" cures because Zola included them, with extraordinary spin doctoring, in his *Lourdes*, a book of five hundred pages in its English translation.

First, fifteen-year-old Clementine Trouvé, who was examined by Dr. Boissarie and nineteen other doctors during the two hours Zola was at the Medical Bureau on August 20. In her twelfth year the child, living in the village of Rouille, France, began to suffer from caries (decay of bone) in the right heel. She came under the care of local Dr. Cibiel, who eventually diagnosed tuberculous osteoperiostitis of the calcaneum. The situation worsened, he operated, and there was a continual flow of matter from a wound that would not heal. She spent four months in Lusignan Hospital. Despite further operations on the heel and the use of detergent injections, there was no improvement. The child left the hospital and could walk only using a crutch. Early in August 1891, Dr. Cibiel probed the wound again while her mother and a Mrs. Sardet restrained the crying child. Much matter still flowed from the wound. On August 10 the head of Lusignan Hospital inspected the wound and found no improvement. The family decided to send Clementine on the Lourdes pilgrimage leaving from nearby Poitiers. Before Clementine was transported to that railhead city, her mother and Mrs. Delaigne and some sympathetic neighbors got her ready, which included putting on fresh bandages. Their signed statement in the dossier at the Lourdes Bureau notes that there was "a gaping wound from which blood and pus were oozing". Also in the dossier is the testimony of Viscountess De G. Roederer, who was in charge of the pilgrimage. Before the pilgrims left Poitiers Railway Station, the viscountess watched while soiled bandages were again removed. She and the volunteer nurses helping the sick pilgrim could see the suppuration had not in any way ceased.

The train pulled into Lourdes on August 20, 1891. They carried Clementine to the *piscines* the next day and put her down outside. A Miss Cornet of Paris and a Mrs. Paul Lallier of Sens escorted her in to be bathed. The two volunteers removed the bandages, and Mrs. Lallier helped the sickly semicripple down the steps into the water, praying aloud to the Virgin as these volunteers usually do. She testified that her prayers were interrupted "because suddenly the child sprang up crying: I am cured, I am cured. . . . At this very moment I saw the wound on her foot closing over before my very eyes! The flesh was actually reuniting itself!"

Clementine, without as much as a thank you to the two volunteers, hastily put on her clothing, picked up her crutch and sped to the nearby Grotto. By the time Mrs. Lallier got there, Clementine had placed the crutch before the Virgin and was pouring out her thanks. The excited volunteer then persuaded Clementine to go with her straight to the Medical Bureau. Dr. Boissarie and the other doctors there listened to Mrs. Lallier's testimony, examined the heel and found only a thin scar—"our Lady's souvenir", as they call it at Lourdes. Almost everyone healed seems to have remaining a small and in no way painful scar or sign of the complaint from which they had suffered. The cured say it keeps fresh forever their gratitude for the grace they received.

Dr. Boissarie told Clementine to report back to the Lourdes Bureau in a year's time if the healing was permanent. He copied out the grim report on the unhealed caries made by Dr. Cibiel just prior to Clementine's leaving on pilgrimage and took down statements by witnesses—the viscountess in charge of the pilgrimage, twenty fellow pilgrims and also Mrs. Lallier. Now, one day short of a year later, Boissarie invited Zola to review the case as the doctors examined the heel. All that remained of the crippling caries was a thin scar. Zola questioned the girl, seemed to be charmed by her, even kissed her. Afterward he accosted Dr. Boissarie sharply: "But you only saw the foot after she left the pool!" The doctor replied, "One thousand sick enter the baths daily. How could we possibly examine them beforehand?" Dr. Boissarie pointed to the sworn statements of people such as the viscountess and Dr. Cibiel's certificate describing the heel immediately prior to the pilgrimage leaving for Lourdes. Then, as Dr. Boissarie stated in his book *L'oeuvre de Lourdes* (Paris, 1907), he challenged Zola to go with him to Clementine's village and meet Cibiel and the girl's parents, neighbors and the head of Lusignan Hospital. The journalists strained against the hubbub in the crowded bureau room to hear Zola's reply. The usually confident author who had told the Paris newspapers he was going "to uncover the whole truth" about Lourdes backed down! He told Dr. Boissarie he didn't have the time. Maybe understandable, unless one remembers he was soon to write much about Clementine in his book on Lourdes.

Zola returned to the Medical Bureau the next day, August 21, 1892, when an excited Marie Lemarchand came in, claiming she had just been "cured". The background, briefly, is this. She was born in the city of Caen, France, the eldest of a large family. In her teens she became sickly and at the age of eighteen was hospitalized in Caen with suspected tuberculosis. They discovered the apex of each lung was tubercular. Large sores began to break out on her body. She was doubly shocked when these ulcers broke out over her face. Dr. La

Marie Lemarchand—Elise Rouquet in Zola's Lourdes.

Neele, the director of the hospital, had the sad duty of telling her she had lupus, a dreaded disease in those days. He did all he could for her, but the tubercular-origin symptoms grew viciously worse. By late July the cheeks, nose and upper lip were a horrible sight, secreting matter continually. She had been coughing up blood for three months at this stage. The fever that came over her nightly indicated, Dr. La Neele thought, that death was fast approaching. Marie sensed this and, despite her weakness and the embarrassment when people saw her hideous face, asked to be taken on the French national pilgrimage leaving for Lourdes just after mid-August. La Neele signed the medical certificate the pilgrimage organizers demanded, outlining her condition—TB in both lungs, coughing blood, ominous fever each night, sores on her body and lupus ulcers on her face "the size of a hand".

The pilgrim train arrived in Lourdes late on the afternoon of August 20, 1892. Marie had a veil over her face and was accompanied by her mother. She was taken to the baths the next day. A Dr. D'hombres happened to be standing close to the entrance and later that day testified at the Medical Bureau. He wrote, "I was struck by her particularly revolting face. Both cheeks, the lower part of her nose and her upper lip were covered with a tuberculous ulcer that secreted matter abundantly."

He remained there, as doctors often do at Lourdes, in case one of the many sick pilgrims needed help. He was still there when she came out of the baths and testified, "I recognized her without difficulty even though her face had changed completely! In place of the hideous ulcer I had just seen, the face was red, it is true, but dry and covered with new skin. . . . The similar sore on her leg had also dried up. . . . I was amazed by this sudden change caused by mere immersion in cold water. I know quite well that lupus is a most difficult disease, resisting every kind of treatment."

Dr. D'hombres went with Marie back to the hospital where she was staying. He then accompanied her to the Medical Bureau. Zola was there with a train of journalists and literary people. D'hombres spoke to Dr. Boissarie, who was overjoyed and said to Zola, "Lo, the case of your dreams!" (Zola had been reported saying, "Only nervous cases are healed at Lourdes. . . . If I saw a cut finger dipped into the water and come out whole I would believe.") Zola was certainly impressed by this case, as he gave it much space in the book he subsequently wrote on Lourdes. However, he did some malicious adjustments to the facts, as will be pointed out later in this chapter.

Marie returned to Caen and presented herself to Dr. La Neele. He wrote and signed the following testimony: "I am quite affected by having had experience of this absolutely supernatural cure. She, without any doubt, suffered from advanced tuberculosis of both lungs with frequently suppurating ulcers on her face and legs. . . . She was suddenly cured by bathing in the Lourdes *piscines*. I saw her immediately on her return [to Caen]. I did not recognize her, she was so changed. I saw a graceful young girl approaching me instead of the mess of humanity with the horrible and monstrous face I had seen ten days previously. The tuberculosis had disappeared." Twelve years later he added, "The cure has lasted!"

Seven years after the cure Marie married and eventually had eight children. You can see a photo of her with her husband and children hanging in the Lourdes Medical Bureau alongside photos of many other famous miracle cases.

That same August 21, Dr. Boissarie introduced Zola to a second impressive case, Marie Lebranchu, a thirty-six-year-old woman from a part of Paris where tuberculosis was common. Both parents had already died of TB when Marie was diagnosed as carrying the dread bacillae. First hospitalized for a time in the Hotel-Dieu under Professor Germain Sée's care, she was later transferred to the Netherlands Hospital for Consumptives in Paris. Ten months later, when she applied to be taken on the August French national pilgrimage to Lourdes (on which Marie Lemarchand was also a pilgrim), her doctor, Dr. Marquezy, wrote a grim report for the pilgrimage organizers: Tuberculous softening and pus in the lung tissue, constantly spitting blood with Koch bacillae, unable to retain food. She had lost forty-eight pounds in weight. The symptoms indicated probable approaching death.

Upon arrival in Lourdes she was taken straight to the *piscines*. The volunteer women on duty wondered about bathing someone in such an emaciated state. However, at her insistence they lowered her into the cold water. Marie emerged cured and was escorted, jubilantly, to the Medical Bureau. Between twenty and thirty doctors were present, and most of them examined her. There was no trace of the disease described in Dr. Marquezy's medical report written in Paris several days before. The doctors called her back to the bureau the following day and found no trace of illness. They also noted that by now she was "eating heartily".

Marie was quite charmed by Zola and all the questions with which he plied her. She told him she would return to her home in Paris, which was in the Rue de Brumelles. That was not too far from where he lived. Would he like to call on her to make sure her cure was perfect? She was sure it was. Zola replied, "Certainly. I shall make a point of it." Marie finished the pilgrimage and returned to Paris. She came the next year to Lourdes on a pilgrimage of thanksgiving and also in 1895 and 1897. She was examined at the Medical Bureau on each occasion and found to be without any trace of TB. Zola did not make good his promise to visit her—even though he made some lengthy and preposterous claims about her subsequent relapse in his book *Lourdes*. She later married, becom-

Marie Lebranchu—La Grivotte in Zola's Lourdes.

ing Mrs. Wuiplier, but was too old to have children. On June 6, 1908, Monsignor Amette, archbishop of Paris, added her name—with those of caries-of-the-heel sufferer Clementine (now Sister Marie Agnes, a nun in the Assumption congregation) and lupus victim Marie Lemarchand—to the list of canonically accepted miracle cures. All three were perfectly well, showing absolutely no symptoms of the old ailments.

Zola's *Lourdes* was published early in 1894. On April 27 he read extracts from it to an enthusiastic crowd of four thousand packed into Paris' Trocadero Palace. That same April the *New York Herald* serialized the English translation. By 1897 the book had sold more copies than any Zola novel except *Nana* and *La Debacle*. The book was a bestseller in spite of—though some thought it was really because of—some glaring falsifications of the evidence presented to Zola at Lourdes. Let me specify them.

Zola devoted many pages in *Lourdes* to Clementine (the young girl with caries of the heel), Marie Lemarchand (lupus) and Marie Lebranchu (TB), giving them the names of, in order, Sophie Couteau, Elise Rouquet and La Grivotte. He provided such detail that anyone who knew the three—such as the Medical Bureau doctors and their fellow pilgrims to Lourdes—could immediately recognize them in the novel. Zola, a leader of the nineteenth-century literary group called Naturalists, followed their style of choosing real persons and actual happenings so as to write as vividly as possible. The pathetic and dramatic pathological state of the three seems to have appealed to Zola, noticeable in the graphic way he wrote about them. He had proved himself a master at this kind of writing, and it won him an extraordinarily large readership in France and beyond.

There are, I believe, other factors present, explaining why Zola took unmistakably real Lourdes cases and blatantly altered them—for example, making Marie Lebranchu go into violent spasms of coughing up blood and die immediately after leaving Lourdes! These factors are his wounded pride and his willfulness. Dr. Boissarie had challenged him and made him back down before journalists and literary folk gathered in the Medical Bureau—daring Zola to travel with him to Clementine Trouvé's hometown to investigate the signed statements about her suppurating caries of the heel. He also had challenged Zola's promise to believe if he saw as much as a cut finger dipped into Lourdes water and healed, by presenting Marie Lemarchand and Marie Lebranchu, on the same day, as examples of far more wonderful organic and instantaneous healing. Zola had been publicly ridiculed. He would publicly ridicule Boissarie, whom he calls Dr. Bonamy in his novel. He despised Dr. Boissarie for his deep Christian beliefs. Zola had written of himself before setting out for Lourdes to gather material for this novel. "What's needed is a man who represents free thought, undogmatic examination, faith only in progress through science, who opposes superstition, who has concluded that Christianity's day is done . . . that it will founder and be replaced." Zola was accustomed to using his immense prestige and fame as a novelist, his wealth and his tremendous willpower to bulldoze through opposition. He seems to have believed these would far outweigh the risk he took in altering the facts about Clementine and the two Maries. He did not think Dr. Boissarie or civic officials from around Lourdes would take him on publicly. He was stunned when they did so, passionately.

Zola made Pierre Froment the hero, and his own spokesman, in the novel. Froment, a priest who eventually lost his faith, said of the testimony given by Sophie (Clementine) about the cure of caries in the heel, "Who knows if she has not slowly and unwittingly distorted the truth? . . . Who knows if the cure was instantaneous or not? After all, no one saw the foot before and after the immersion in the *piscines*." Zola knew this was untrue. Mrs. Lallier, the volunteer nurse in the *piscines*, Viscountess Roederer and a score of fellow pilgrims—not to mention Clementine's family, the head of the Lusignan Hospital and Dr. Cibiel—had left signed statements to contradict this. Zola had refused Dr. Boissarie's challenge to travel with him to meet them all.

Next is the case of Marie Lemarchand, the eighteen-year-old girl with lupus. Zola called her Elise Rouquet in his book, describing Marie's hideous face exactly, though omitting the TB in her lungs and the large sores on her body. The real Marie Lemarchand was healed instantaneously, as Dr. D'hombres, an eyewitness, testified. Zola had Elise Rouquet, his puppet, "bathing her face repeatedly since the morning". In the late afternoon "it seemed to her the raw flesh was beginning to dry and grow paler . . . and less horrible. . . . The next day the lupus was showing signs of cure. . . . She continued bathing her face at the miraculous fountain. . . . The face was displaying symptoms of a gradual cure."

Finally, Zola had his mouthpiece, Pierre Froment, say solemnly: "Our most learned medical men suspect many of these sores to be of nervous origin . . . some are beginning to prove that faith which heals can even cure sores, certain forms of lupus among them." What researchers of the time actually were saying, mainly under the impetus of the great neurologist Charcot of the Salpêtrière, was that some sicknesses "of hysterical origin" could be cured by religious "faith", Christian and otherwise, and by hypnosis. A foremost scientist in this field at that time was Hippolyte Bernheim. (Freud came to France to consult him in 1889.) Bernheim in his *Treatise on Hypnotism* stated explicitly that "organic lesions cannot be cured by hypnotism".[1] Zola's "most learned medical men" were simply pulled out of his hat!

The writer Joris-Karl Huysmans had once been a dedicated disciple and personal friend of Zola, and fellow unbeliever. He came to distrust Zola's grand theories about humanity, and their ways parted. Huysmans, too, became a leading French writer. His last book was *The Crowds of Lourdes*, based on his personal research there.[2] It was also a deliberate response to Zola's novel. Huysmans described in detail many instantaneous cures of thoroughly organic diseases. Of Zola's treatment of Marie Lemarchand's cure from lupus he wrote: "Zola invented stages and degrees so as not to be compelled to confess that this sudden restoration of a ruined face was beyond the laws of nature. . . . The story as told by Zola is deliberately inaccurate." Even if one accepted

[1] H. Bernheim, *Suggestive Therapeutics: A Treatise on the Nature and Uses of Hypnotism*, English translation from 2nd rev. ed. (New York: G. P. Putnam's Sons, 1889).

[2] Joris-Karl Huysmans, *The Crowds of Lourdes*, translated by W. H. Mitchell (London: Burns, Oates and Co. 1925).

Joris Karl Huysmans (1848–1907).

Zola's totally unwarranted statement that Marie's lupus was of nervous origin, Huysmans added, the instantaneous restoration of cells and tissues is against the physical laws clearly known to medical scientists.

He attacked Zola's use of slogans as if they were explanations, such as this one: "The healing inspiration of a crowd and its unknown power". Huysmans replied, in words similar to those Nobel Prize winner Alexis Carrel would later use of Lourdes miracles, "The unknown power has a name, prayer . . . and often prayer at a great distance from Lourdes, as in many well-researched cases like that of de Rudder, far away in Belgium, who simply prayed to Our Lady of Lourdes."

Finally Huysmans suggested a powerful reason why Zola was dead-set "against recognizing prayer and the supernatural". Accepting Christ "would mean giving up illicit pleasures of the flesh". This reflection came from his association with Zola when he was younger.

Then there was Zola's treatment of Marie Lebranchu, unmistakably the model of his La Grivotte in the book. Zola's spokesman was again Pierre Froment, the priest who eventually lost his faith but continued his ministry. (France was full of such sham priests, asserted Zola.) Father Pierre had been stunned to see the extraordinary improvement of La Grivotte "exulting" in the Medical Bureau after leaving the *piscines*. She was no longer the dying wreck he saw in the pilgrim train the day before. Next day they left together by train for Paris. Hardly had the trip begun than La Grivotte began spitting blood by the "throatful", going ashen and collapsing. The train had gone only as far as Bordeaux when La Grivotte's life was ebbing fast. The stationmaster took her off to a Bordeaux hospital to die. This was obscene caricature. The real Marie Lebranchu was completely freed of TB and outlived Zola by many years.

Zola's book sold quickly and immediately went into translations around the globe. Dr. Boissarie acted as soon as it came out, writing to Zola and accusing him of lying and challenging him to a debate with himself and eyewitnesses of the miracle stories he had falsified. Zola did not reply. Dr. Boissarie was kept away from Paris as busy medical director at Lourdes. However, eventually he could go to Paris. The Lourdes official pilgrimage season ends in October with winter's arrival. With the help of a Catholic group called "the Luxembourg Circle", Dr. Boissarie set up a public meeting in Paris, on November 21, 1894. Fifteen hundred people attended, among them Bishop Peri-Morozoni, many Catholic doctors and lawyers and journalists from both left and right newspapers. Dr. Boissarie was the main speaker and put twelve people on the stage who had been healed at Lourdes of organic diseases. One of them was Marie Lebranchu. Boissarie described her instantaneous healing of lupus—and then read out Zola's travestied account. The journalists wrote up the meeting next day. Zola met the grave charges with silence!

The following year an exasperated Dr. Boissarie traveled to Paris again, stormed into Zola's home and accused him of gross lying about Lourdes miracles. The author retorted that a novelist is free to create characters as he wishes. True, responded Boissarie, "but not the right to falsify history!"

"La Grivotte did not die at Bordeaux", he said. "She is alive and well, and I can take you to her." Again the author dodged a Boissarie challenge. The doctor returned to Lourdes angry that so many people believed Lourdes was a big fake because of the bad faith of this best-selling author.

Dr. Boissarie was in for further disenchantment. Marie Lebranchu wrote to him in Lourdes telling him that some days after he burst in on Zola, the latter had come to visit her. He promised the woman and her laborer husband that if they agreed to go and live in Belgium they would never want financially. She told Dr. Boissarie she was momentarily tempted. Her husband was not always sure of a job, and her long hours working in the Bon Marché department store brought in precious little. Dr. Boissarie quoted her letter in *L'oeuvre de Lourdes*, which devotes a whole chapter to Zola's *Lourdes* and his altering of the facts.

Another man who responded to Zola's book about Lourdes was Paris' Archbishop Amette. On June 6, 1908, he announced the conclusions of his own investigation into the cures of Clementine Trouvé's heel and those of the two Maries. He declared them certainly miraculous, to be inscribed among the official canonical cures. On that occasion he asked Marie Lebranchu if she was prepared to swear under oath that Zola had visited her home with a money offer trying to persuade both her and her husband to disappear, taking up residence in Belgium. She swore that oath.

Use of the media for disinformation on Lourdes has not ended. In 1995 Frederick Brown, a professor at the State University of New York, Stony Brook, brought out his 888-page *Zola: A Life*. The Guggenheim Foundation and the National Endowment for the Humanities had awarded Brown endowments to research and write the book. I read it from cover to cover and found it fascinating, magnificently researched and even gigantic in its vision of the history, literature and general culture of Zola's France. I also discovered an author who shares in Zola's intense dislike of Catholicism. That is his right. Some Catholics have done and continue to do much that needs to be criticized. However, I was deeply perturbed that while he gives considerable detail about Zola's book *Lourdes*, he has absolutely nothing on the public and sustained challenges to Zola's truthfulness as I have outlined earlier. The three falsified miracles, Zola's attempt to bribe Marie Lebranchu, the challenges to Zola by the Luxembourg Circle meeting, by Dr. Boissarie, by professor of philosophy M. Rousseil and many others who went into print, including secular journalists at the time—none of this gets a mention in Brown's monumental work. The otherwise meticulous biographer contents himself to note Catholic anger at Zola's book and merely quotes Zola's self-justification: "What they [the Catholics] can't forgive is my laying bare all the secret dramas of Lourdes . . . all the little mysteries unveiled: That's the real explanation of all this anger." As G. K. Chesterton would say, "Chuck it, Brown!"

Chapter 15

FATIMA, 1917

Miracle of the Sun

I SPENT THREE MONTHS in 1997 going to the main Marian pilgrim shrines, researching instantaneous healing of serious physical illness. A travel company announced that year that religious shrines are now the most frequented destination of travelers to Europe. Lourdes draws 5.5 million yearly, Fatima nearly as many. Saint Padre Pio's shrine at Rotondo in Italy is visited by 7.5 million annually, according to *The Tablet* (October 3, 1998). The shrine of the Black Madonna at Czestochowa in Poland draws 3.5 million each year. Rue du Bac in Paris, shrine of the Miraculous Medal, averages between 2.2 and 2.5 million. Knock in Ireland draws 1.5 million, while Guadalupe in Mexico City, a pilgrim shrine since 1531, now averages 13 million pilgrims annually.

Lourdes is a place of great beauty. There are majestic mountains to the south, snowcapped even in early summer. The rushing waters of the Gave are a delight to behold, and in summer the Lourdes valleys are carpeted with lush pastures, crops and wildflowers. God chose a beautiful site for this oasis of the spirit.

Fatima is very different. The rugged uplands surrounding Fatima are burdened with stones, like so much of Israel, and yield grudging harvests and stunted trees. Freezing winter storms come howling down from the north, while the summer heat can be debilitating.

The six Fatima apparitions occurred in 1917, when the world was bogged down in what seemed to have become a winless and suicidal war in French and Flemish trenches. The children seers were told by "the Lady" that war comes from flouting God's laws. The present war would soon end, she said. However, if people did not amend their lives, a worse war would follow, and Russia would spread falsehood and destruction on a global scale. This warning about Russia came just before Lenin left his hideaway hut in Finland to enter Petrograd on October 20 and launch the Communist revolution. Many fascinating books have been written about the Fatima prophecies of a worse war and Russia-led conquests. However, the main purpose of this book is to help unbelievers or wobbly believers come to certitude about a personal and loving God at work to save our present times. I will therefore concentrate on one momentous event at Fatima—the prediction, made three months beforehand by "the Lady" and repeated by the children, of a "miracle so that everyone can believe". It would take place at noon on October 13, stated the Lady several times.

One reason why Fatima, an uncomfortable place off the beaten track, draws five million pilgrims yearly is a series of thoroughly researched books by some top-flight authors that came out at the time of, or immediately after, the forewarned "worse war", 1939–1945. The horror of that war shocked those writers into a special interest in Fatima. As thirty years had not passed since the events, most key witnesses were still alive and very ready to give witness about October 13.

One of these writers was William T. Walsh, a historian and teacher with special competence concerning the Iberian peninsula. His knowledge of the Spanish and Portuguese languages enabled him to do direct research. His scholarly 1930 tome *Isabella* won him international standing. This was followed by *Philip II*, and then the spiritual and historical classic *Saint Teresa of Avila*. After World War II, when the West began to take Fatima seriously, he made several trips to Portugal to research it thoroughly, communicating directly with the many eyewitnesses still living. His classic *Our Lady of Fatima* came out in 1947.[1]

The Oxford don C. C. Martindale, S.J., convert and widely known writer, broadcaster and lecturer on both sides of the Atlantic, spent sixty vigorous years preaching and explaining the Catholic faith. He had to be careful of his facts, or he would have become open game to academics and journalists who did not share his convictions. This priest made several research trips to Fatima and was greatly helped by the painstaking investigations carried out by a fellow Jesuit in the early 1940s. This was the Portuguese G. da Fonseca, a professor at Rome's prestigious Biblical Institute. Da Fonseca's seminal study came out in 1943. Father Martindale's *The Message of Fatima* also drew on *Vision of Fatima*, by priest-sculptor Thomas McGlynn, O.P. The latter had many long interviews with the chief seer, by then a nun, as he created his well-known sculpture of Our Lady of Fatima. McGlynn's book was published in 1951. Eight years earlier another Dominican, Archbishop F. Ryan—helped by his sister, the Irish academic Dr. Mary Ryan—had published his *Our Lady of Fatima*. The archbishop was able to recheck original docu-

---

[1] William T. Walsh, *Our Lady of Fatima* (New York: Macmillan, 1947; repr. Doubleday Image Book, 1954).

ments with the help of his friend Jose da Silva, bishop of the Fatima area since 1920. Bishop da Silva's archives had the very precise documents drawn up by Dr. Manoel Formigao, who had been an eyewitness of the last three apparitions and had been officially appointed to interrogate the three seers. He witnessed the ten- to twelve-minute "miracle of the sun" on October 13, 1917.

John I. Haffert has spent most of his adult years deeply interested in Fatima. He personally interviewed two hundred eyewitnesses of the "sun miracle". He quoted them at length in his book, published in 1961, *Meet the Witnesses*. Professor J. M. Alonso of the theology faculty at Catholic University, Lisbon, brought out a seventeen-volume work on all aspects of Fatima—its history, message and literature—between 1967 and 1976.

Many people have denied the sun miracle because "miracles cannot happen". None of them has given, however, a credible explanation of what well over seventy thousand people witnessed on October 13, 1917.

First, a brief overview of the Fatima events. On May 13, 1917, three children who had taken the family flock of sheep out to graze, as they did every day, were startled by an apparition of a "most beautiful young woman". She asked them to come to this same spot at noon on the thirteenth of each month until October. That was noon, solar time. As poor peasants they had no watches but had learned the shepherds' knack of judging the time. The eldest of the children was ten, young by Western city standards. However, as Father Martindale discovered from observing them, young Portuguese farm children were given serious responsibilities that brought on initiative and maturity quickly. Martindale also emphasized Jesus' insistence on the vital importance of developing a childlike heart if one wishes to make it to heaven. Martindale saw profound gospel symbolism in heaven's choice of young

Bernadette and the Fatima children. If this is an affront to the sophistication of the affluent West, maybe this is deliberately so, a powerful gospel lesson itself!

Lucia Santos cautioned her two younger companions, her cousins Francisco Marto and his sister Jacinta, to remain silent about the heavenly Lady; but Jacinta could not hold her tongue. When the story got back to Maria Rosa, Lucia's mother, she ordered her daughter to confess to making the story up. Lucia assured her it was true and received a thrashing. If there was one thing Maria Rosa abhorred in her children it was lying in any form. "Ti" Marto, father of Francisco and Jacinta, listened to the story thoughtfully and held his peace. He was the only family member to do so. The others decided it was make-believe.

Maria Rosa hoped Lucia would forget it all by June 13, fiesta of Saint Anthony of Padua, a time of fun, games and feasting for adults and children in the whole area. Lucia and her two young cousins, however, marched steadfastly off to the Lady's rendezvous site, turning their backs on the fiesta. About fifty adults turned up, too—none of them from the children's family or village. They were deeply impressed by the demeanor of the children.

The parish priest, Marques Ferreira, was understandably disturbed as the fifty witnesses enthusiastically told everyone of the "apparition of our Lady". Portugal was in the throes of an anti-Catholic persecution. The king had been assassinated in 1908 by revolutionaries who held to the same antimonarchy, anti-Catholic program as the instigators of the French Revolution in 1789. By 1910 the new Republican government had disbanded the Jesuits and most religious orders, imprisoned or exiled leading clergy, confiscated church property and told the remaining parish priests what they could preach and what they could not. They forbade wearing clerical clothing in public. Freemason Grand Master

Magahaes Lima stated triumphantly that "no Portuguese would want to become a priest within a few years". To hasten this prediction, the theology faculty at the famous thirteenth-century Coimbra University was dissolved.

Some of the anger against Catholicism and the priesthood was, as in the French Revolution, resentment for clerical privileges. Priests, part of the royal establishment, were regarded as aristocrats and often acted like them. The persecution and removal of privileges did priests and religious a service, forcing them to live more like the poor Galilean. However, the anticlerical government was committed to Catholicism's disappearance. In 1910 the minister of justice in the new Republican government, Alfonso Costa, announced, "Catholicism, the main cause of Portugal's present wretchedness, could be extinguished within two generations."

The Republicans found it much harder to recruit enthusiasts for their anti-Catholic program in the rural areas than in the cities. The Fatima story was first spread among and by rural folk, who fervently hoped this was a response from heaven to the government's antisupernaturalism.

As with the French Revolution, when the Girondin and Jacobin allies began to turn on each other, the Portuguese Republicans soon split and fought each other murderously. From 1910 to 1926, sixteen bloody revolutions broke out, and the nation went though eight changes of president. Fatima pastor Father Ferreira had been watching all this violence and anti-Catholicism with apprehension. He was the last person to welcome "apparitions" to rough, uneducated children. Catholicism was barely surviving. This apparition nonsense would only stir the civil officials to new attacks. He met the enthusiastic reports of witnesses of the June 13 apparition with aloofness and coldness. When pressed about the extraordinary conviction of the eyewitnesses, he remarked that Satan was adept at working tricks. This was all

Lucia's mother needed to hear. She was a woman under a lot of strain at the time. Her husband, Antonio, was drinking through the family finances, selling off pieces of farmland to pay the wine shop. To add to his absenteeism from farm work, their only son had been called up by the army and was being trained for action in those highly dangerous French trenches. She had become thoroughly run down, and the medicine the doctor gave her for her heart condition was bringing no relief. Now, to cap all her woes, her youngest child, who should have been her consolation, was lying about sacred things and, said Father Ferreira, was possibly being used by Satan! She dragged Lucia off to the presbytery, where the daughter further infuriated parent and priest by refusing to budge one inch about the beautiful Lady appearing to her in May and June.

More than two thousand people surrounded the three children at the July 13 apparition. The messages the children relayed to the people afterward were about prayer, especially saying the Rosary. Again the bystanders were impressed by the demeanor of the children. However, the huge crowd increased the hostility of Lucia's family, especially of her father, Antonio, by trampling much of his ploughed fields. Her whole family again berated her angrily. There was a new turn to the messages, however. When Lucia complained that her family and many others were treating her as a liar, the Lady promised a miracle on October 13 "so that all would believe". Now here was a public challenge, a prophecy in detail as to day and hour. This delighted the believers, who spread the word far and wide to towns and cities.

The Republican government in Lisbon ordered the administrator of the whole area, Artur Santos, to put a stop to the reactionary nonsense. Santos was an ex-blacksmith who had espoused the Rationalist cause with a passion and energy that brought quick promotion in civil administration. He had named his three children Democracy, Republic and Liberty! The glorious goals of the New Republic justified in his mind disregarding the civil rights of its enemies. He once, for instance, jailed six priests and held them incommunicado for eight days. He was quite sure similar direct action would scotch this Fatima superstition.

He turned up in Fatima early on August 13 and visited the children, professing deep interest "in these supernatural matters". He said he would personally escort them to the apparition site in his own horse-drawn vehicle. He managed to get the reluctant three children aboard and sped them off to Ourem, seven and one-half miles southwest of Fatima, where he lived. In the meantime, upward of five thousand people gathered at the apparition site.

Confident he could intimidate the children, Santos took them to his administration office and with several officials began threatening them. When they held fast he had them taken off one by one to be "boiled in oil". The children believed him and made tearful farewells to each other but showed no sign of wavering. Next he transferred them to his jailhouse, a large cell holding a collection of petty criminals. The children surprised the latter by inviting them to kneel and say the Rosary—which they did!

On August 15 Santos had the children transported back to Fatima and dumped at the presbytery. He knew the priest had already called them liars. The imprisonment had terrified Lucia's family and hardened her mother's opposition to her daughter's "fabrications". However, most of the five thousand-plus who had gathered for the August 13 apparition began speaking of Jesus' predictions that his disciples would be persecuted, "imprisoned and hauled before judges". They spread the Fatima story, and the promise of the miracle on October 13, with enthusiasm. The three children, as Father Martindale points out, were remarkably independent and strong-willed. They were not shaken by their kidnapping and imprisonment, only disappointed they had not been there for the August 13 rendezvous with the Lady. She reassured them, however, by appearing on August 19 while they tended their sheep, lamenting the wickedness of the civil authorities and reiterating her promise of a miracle on October 13. The children quietly repeated this to the many who were traveling to Fatima to question them.

The Fatima events were now being discussed all over Portugal. The nation's biggest daily newspaper, the Rationalist leaning *O Seculo*, ran an article attacking the "psychosis, epilepsy and collective suggestion" at the root of the "medieval reactionism". Jose do Vale, editor of another Rationalist newspaper, *O Mundo*, went to the expense of printing pamphlets denouncing this "Jesuits and priests" ploy, calling on "friends of progress and enlightenment" to put a stop to it. In point of fact most priests, barely tolerated by the government in what had now become a cold war, were fearful the Fatima events could worsen the fragile situation. They told parishioners who asked them that in all probability it was yet another case of hallucination and to put no credence in the whole affair. One Lisbon priest, Father Cruz, decided to go to Fatima to interview the children. He remembered Lucia very well from having given her First Communion some years before. The pastor had refused her, saying that at age seven she was too young. She had come tearfully to Father Cruz, who was giving a mission to the Fatima parish. She told him she knew all her catechism, and he found this was very true when he examined her. Impressed by her mature answers, he persuaded the parish priest to allow her to receive Communion. Though quite unwell, he now made the difficult trip to Fatima and questioned her and the two other seers at length. He returned to Lisbon, where he was highly regarded as a saintly spiritual director, and told people he believed the apparitions were genuine.

Cardinal Belo, patriarch of Lisbon and the nation's senior churchman, was still out of the country, exiled by the government. His administrator probably heard about Father Cruz's favorable impression. In any case, the Fatima affair was now too talked about to ignore, so he ordered two qualified priests to investigate things firsthand at the coming September 13 "apparition". One was his vicar-general, Monsignor Quaresma, the other Dr. Manoel Formigao, canon of the cathedral and a professor at Santarem seminary.

Thirty thousand people were present for September 13. The vast majority of them and the two priests from Lisbon were deeply impressed. On September 27 Dr. Formigao returned to interview the three children—separately, to see if their accounts were the same. The Lady had again prophesied a great miracle on October 13 to convince doubters. By now Lucia's family and some relatives of the other two children, Francisco and Jacinta Marto, were beginning to panic, fearing what an angry mob might do to the children, and to themselves, when no miracle took place. The two families were being advised to spirit the children away into hiding. The father of the Marto children, who was a very forceful character, retained serene faith the miracle would take place and put a stop to all talk of whisking the children away.

Dr. Formigao was not receiving much credence from fellow priests. It all sounded like a childish aping of Lourdes. Formigao came to Fatima again on October 11. He queried the parents as to whether the children had previously shown particular interest in stories of apparitions like Lourdes. He was told no. He found Lucia's family terrified, sure there would be no miracle. When he raised the matter with Lucia herself, she showed no nervousness or hesitancy. The Lady had promised a miracle, so it would take place. The younger two exhibited the same supreme confidence.

The parish priest of Mos, Father Pocas, also turned up,

with a male parishioner, and proceeded to castigate the children fiercely. He said he knew it was all a hoax. If they did not admit it to him now, he was going to denounce them publicly as impostors before October 13. When he failed to move the children one inch, his parishioner took over. He told them they were guilty of the terrible sin of "witchcraft". The children quietly replied that everyone would understand when the Lady worked her miracle on the thirteenth.

An icy wind swept down on the uplands around Fatima on October 12. Mists rolled in, and then fine rain fell. By nightfall a big crowd had already squatted down in Cova da Iria, the saucer-shaped area where the apparitions took place. Their umbrellas were no match for the wind-whipped rain, but people showed no inclination to move. Many were peasants who had walked several days to get there.

They hardly realized dawn had broken on October 13, so heavy were the clouds. Then the rain began to fall in torrents. Soon the ground was a quagmire, yet none yielded their prized positions, despite the misery of wet trousers, dresses

The crowd gathering in anticipation of October 13, 1917, Fatima.

and blankets around their shoulders. A continual drone of the Rosary went up. The well-to-do sat in cars around the perimeter.

By midmorning a cross section of unbelievers had come, too. There was Avelino de Almeida, for instance, manager/editor of the big daily *O Seculo*. That morning's edition carried his cynical article about the miracle that unsophisticated people thought would happen. The article did admit approvingly that most priests had given no encouragement whatsoever to the Fatima frenzy. The edition also carried a crude cartoon: The only "apparition" would be the very real hunger of the impoverished! De Almeida, his photographer and other journalists had come to get firsthand material for articles about the nonevent prophecy that would put an end to Fatima.

Some academics were there, too. One can see from their statements after the event that some of them had all but lost the faith but had lingering, nostalgic hopes that Christ and the Virgin might possibly be real.

By midday, watch time, the vast saucer depression was packed with people. Professor Almeida Garrette of Coimbra University thought there must be one hundred thousand. Conservative estimates made it seventy thousand. When his watch hand passed 12 noon, one man dressed as a priest began to shout that it was all a hoax, and he attempted to hustle the three children away. The latter refused to go, saying the Lady would keep her promise. The doubter received little support from the crowd. Later efforts to identify him failed, and it seems he was not a priest but a government agent.

About an hour or so later, when it was noon, solar time, Lucia called out, "Put down your umbrellas." Most in the crowd obeyed, despite the rain. The three children went into their ecstatic state.

After some time Lucia called out, though she did not later

Newspaper photo of people looking at the sun phenomenon,
Fatima, October 13, 1917.

remember doing so, "Look at the sun!" Faces turned up to
the sky, and, while they watched, the rain ceased and the
heavy clouds parted. The sun appeared, shining brilliantly,
but people could look at it directly without the slightest
eyestrain! For the next ten to twelve minutes, witnesses later
testified, the sun went through an extraordinary series of
gyrations. The reluctant but honest editor de Almeida wrote
in O Seculo on Monday, October 15, "The sun began to
dance", and he described it. First it whirled around like
those firecrackers called Catherine Wheels. Then it zigzagged erratically across the sky. Rays of light, the colors of
the spectrum, began to fly out from the sun, bathing people
and landscape in alternating colors.

Professor Garrette related that he was one hundred yards
away from the crowd, up on rising ground. He had been
"calm and cold, with curiosity dying down because nothing

had happened. . . . Then I heard the roar of a thousand voices and saw the multitude look up at the sky." He described how he looked directly at the sun, without his eyes hurting. The sun had become "a disc spinning dizzily around . . . whirling on itself with mad rapidity".

Suddenly everything became a purple color. Fearing his eyesight had been affected, Professor Garrette covered his eyes with his hands. When he looked again, the whole scene was still bathed in purple. "Just after that I heard a peasant standing near me exclaim, 'That lady is yellow!' as the dominant color changed again. Next," he continued, "the sun, now blood red, still whirling at great speed, detached itself from the firmament and dropped threateningly, as if to crush us with the weight of its vast and fiery mass. These moments made a terrifying impression."

In his *O Seculo* article on October 15, Avelino de Almeida, writing of the phenomenon of the startling colors shooting out from the sun and its "dancing with abrupt movements", admitted these happenings were "outside all cosmic laws". He was bitterly attacked by fellow freethinkers for writing that article.

Several days later, *Illustracao Portuguesa* carried a dramatic photo of people looking up at the sun with astonished faces. The Lisbon newspaper *O Dia* ran a similar article on October 17, describing the phenomenon in words like de Almeida's. A similar article by a Domingos Coelho appeared in the newspaper *Orden*. These newspaper articles, and their dramatic photos of the sodden crowd, first under a roof of umbrellas and then with umbrellas down and looking up at the sky, had a tremendous impact on Portugal. These newspapers, until then following the Republican government's antichurch line, had been anything but friendly to the Catholic cause. They had sent journalists precisely to write articles about the failure of the miracle prophecy.

Carlos Mendes was a lawyer who, though only twenty-eight years of age, ran the municipal office at Torres Novas and would later be elected to the national parliament. He went to Fatima on October 13 because his brother, on leave from the fighting in France, badgered him to drive him there. He described the solar events in language similar to that already quoted by the other eyewitnesses. He noted in particular the reaction of the people, who were terrified when "the sun, having turned into what seemed a crown of fire, spinning on itself and moving across the sky", began to plummet to earth. Most of the crowd knelt in prayer, many praying aloud, he noted.

One youth, who was to become Father Ignatius Pereira, sat in a village school about six miles away from Fatima. His teacher rushed out of their classroom, followed by the pupils, when a roar went up from villagers outside the school. They stood transfixed, gaping at the antics of the sun, and most became terrified when it zigzagged and came plummeting down. He remembered one unbeliever who had earlier been jeering at the people going off to Fatima. He wrote, "Now he stood there as if paralyzed, stunned, staring at the heavens. I then saw him shake from head to foot, raise his hands to heaven and fall on his knees in the mud crying, 'Holy Virgin, Holy Virgin'." This testimony appeared in Professor G. da Forseca's 1943 book about Fatima.

Joaquim Lourenco, who later became a priest and a canon lawyer in the diocese of Leiria, was a pupil at the same school. He witnessed the sun spectacle with Pereira, their teacher and the whole school. He and Pereira are featured in John Haffert's book *Meet the Witnesses*, two of the two hundred witnesses personally interviewed by Haffert in the course of his research.

Later on that October 13, Dr. Formigao went to the children's homes and interviewed them, again separately, about what the Lady had said. He had witnessed the phenomenon of October 13 and told fellow priests what he had seen. Their first reaction was quite negative. One retorted that it was obviously a case of crowd hysteria and mass hallucination. However, Formigao pointed out that no one had been expecting a solar miracle; no one was even thinking about it. He was soon able to quote people in distant villages who saw the phenomenon independently of any links with the crowd. A number of these would eventually testify in print. A well-known Portuguese author, the Marquis de Cruz, published *The Virgin of Fatima* in 1937. He first quoted eye-witnesses who were at Fatima on October 13, among them his own sister. Then he quoted "the brilliant poet Alfonso Lopes Viera", with whom he visited the evening of October 30, 1935, on the balcony of the poet's home in San Pedro der Muel, thirty miles from Fatima. "On October 13, 1917, I had forgotten about the prediction of the three shepherd children when I was surprised and charmed by a spectacle in the skies", Viera told de Cruz. "It was truly astounding, and I've never so much as heard of anything similar to what I watched from this balcony." The Marquis added, "Dozens and dozens of people of absolute trustworthiness, whom I've known intimately from childhood, as well as people from various parts of Portugal who were present, have testified to seeing the great miracle."

The miracle was obviously worked in the senses of the people who watched the phenomenon. Had the sun really performed like that for ten to twelve minutes, the solar system would have been thrown into chaos! Worldwide observatories would have recorded it. Furthermore, had the phenomenon occurred because of some strange play of light, all would have seen the same things, but they didn't. Some did not see all the colored lights, for instance. The Jesuit scientist Pio Sciatizzi worked at unearthing some possible natural explanation. There was none, he said. He concluded that the solar phenomenon foretold on a number of occasions from three months beforehand, with the date and the noontime hour specified, was "the most obvious and colossal miracle in history". He meant observed miracles, of course. Scripture's miracles, such as the Resurrection, were not observed while happening.

Some freethinkers hit back rather clumsily. During the night of October 23–24, members of the Masonic Lodge of Santarem raided the small oratory set up by layfolk in the field where the apparitions had taken place. They carried off the two crosses, the statue of Mary and the lanterns and put them on show in a building close to the seminary in Santarem. The next night they held a mock procession in the streets, parodying Catholic prayers, litanies and hymns. The blasphemies backfired, and protests poured in. The previously unfriendly newspaper *O Seculo* denounced the crudity and the blatant unfairness. Catholics, who made up the bulk of the population, were forbidden public processions, though these involved no attacks on anyone. Hostile anti-Catholics, however, were allowed to parade at will!

The Portuguese Federation of Freethinkers responded by putting out pamphlets attacking the Fatima story as a brazen plot of "reactionaries" organized "for commercial purposes". The "miracle" was merely a case of "simple folk ingeniously deceived by collective suggestion". The Freethinkers called for a vigorous campaign to uphold "Truth, Reason and Science" against "the pernicious propaganda of the reactionaries' fanaticism, superstition . . . and credulity. . . . Let us liberate ourselves not only from foolish beliefs in such gross and laughable tricks as Fatima, but more especially from any credence in the supernatural and in an alleged God omnipotent, omniscient and omni-everything, instrument of the subtle imagination of rogues who want to capture popular credulity for their own purposes."

The Catholic position took a turn for the better in December 1917, when President Sindono Pais recalled Cardinal Belo from exile. However, Pais was assassinated less than a year later. After December 1918 the new national government decided the Fatima saga must end. Armed guards were sent to the site to curtail the growing cult.

The local Catholics, with the timorous parish priest still refusing to get interested or involved, had built a small pilgrimage chapel. The sculptor Jose Ferreira Theadim was approached to carve a statue of Our Lady of Fatima. He came, consulted Lucia and became an enthusiastic believer in the apparitions. His exquisite statue, which he carved on his knees as an act of devotion to Mary, became the "pilgrim statue" that would eventually tour the world and be duplicated in many hundreds of churches and shrines. Most find it an effective work of art, capturing Mary's goodness, and sadness, as she pleads for twentieth-century neo-pagans to return to God, proclaiming that only conversion from sin will banish world wars. The statue was placed in the chapel in early May 1920. Lucia cried for happiness when she saw it unveiled.

Pilgrims had increased greatly through 1919. Administrator Santos, who jailed the children without a warrant three years before, received curt instructions from the central government. The minister of the interior told him "the mystification at Fatima must stop. People who do not follow this instruction must be prosecuted."

To prevent any ceremony on May 13, Santos stationed a large number of armed troops around the site. A huge crowd of pilgrims came, and an angry confrontation was brewing. The parish priest was nowhere to be seen! Dr. Formigao stepped into the breach and talked the crowd into returning home peacefully. One of the armed guards moved over to thank him, telling him how he hated his job: Our Lady of Fatima had saved his sister's life.

Despite the prohibition, pilgrims kept coming to pray. The statue was on display during the day but was hidden in someone's home each night. The bishop had already weathered the worst that government jails had to offer and held them in no fear. He did fear, however, the harm that a careless acceptance of Fatima could cause to his already battered people. Like the bishop of Lourdes in 1858, he set up a commission of experts, seven in the case of Fatima, to investigate the whole affair painstakingly. Complete thoroughness rather than speed was asked for. Reported healings were studied, and sound judgments on healings are never hurried. It takes time to know if the healings are permanent.

The commission handed the bishop their findings on April 14, 1929. He took more time for his own investigations of this report and subsequent developments. On October 13, 1930, his statement was promulgated before one hundred thousand pilgrims at Fatima. The visions of the children were worthy of belief, and devotion to Our Lady of Fatima was officially authorized in his diocese.

For me and for millions, including John Paul II, the Fatima apparitions are facts. They mean this: God is real; he loves us and is deeply concerned about our salvation. Through Mary he repeats his Son's message: Death will usher us into heavenly life with him if we have lived lovingly and tried hard to avoid evil. Fatima says life is "for keeps"—as boys playing marbles used to put it. When life is almost over, we cannot grab our marbles from the ring and go home. We never really had a home that was ours, or marbles!

A closing note: There are minor discrepancies in the Fatima story, such as when World War I would end and about the child in Purgatory. Minor discrepancies are not surprising, given the shouting crowd of mostly unsophisticated people surrounding the children after the apparitions. Some words become garbled when speeding from mouth to

mouth. There are also minor discrepancies in the three Gospel accounts of the Resurrection, but the essentials of the
event are clear.

Chapter 16

HEALING FIRE FROM FROZEN EARTH

BERNADETTE SOUBIROUS was born in 1844, the eldest child of parents deeply in love. Their love flowed out to Bernadette and her siblings. It was one of the few sustaining constants in an upbringing that would soon be progressively erratic and grim.

Bernadette was plump and healthy until the age of six, when she developed asthma. It would trouble her for the rest of her life. Her parents had begun married life prosperously, running a good flour mill. However, they entertained customers too well, did not keep an eye on the books or chase up payments and allowed equipment like flour sieves to deteriorate. Their flour slipped in quality, customers decreased, and, finally, unable to pay the rent on the mill, they had to vacate it. With a deep sense of shame the family moved into a dilapidated lodging, and the parents were forced to become "casuals", seeking any jobs available. Bernadette's mother began going to homes to do washing and cleaning. That was 1854, when Bernadette was ten and a half. At the end of that year, Pope Pius IX proclaimed Mary's Immaculate Conception—through the foreseen merits of Christ, Mary was conceived in her mother's womb without those human defects summed up under "original sin". By that December the Soubirous family was too busy grubbing desperately to feed their four children to attend the parish celebration of the Immaculate Conception. With the parents hiring themselves out for casual work, Bernadette had to mind the little ones all day. Having had no regular schooling, she was illiterate and could not speak proper French. She spoke only the local patois called Bigorre.

In the autumn of 1855 a cholera epidemic swept through the Bigorre valleys, killing many children. Bernadette contracted the dreaded disease and was left with a permanently weakened constitution. Medical expenses worsened her parents' financial position.

In 1857 Bernadette's parents were unable to pay the rent on their dilapidated lodgings and were literally thrown out onto the streets. A cousin took pity and allowed the six Soubirous to move into a thirteen-by-eight-foot room in the "Cachot" (jail). The grim building had been condemned as unsanitary by the authorities and sold to this cousin. The storeroom he gave the family was damp and icy in winter and a breezeless, stifling place in summer. The acrid smell from the big manure heap directly outside was an all-year affair. Bernadette's asthma worsened in the Cachot.

On March 27, 1857, two gendarmes startled and terrified the children by executing a search warrant in the Cachot. Two bags of flour had been stolen from the Maisongrosse Bakery. Bernadette's father, who had done casual work there, was a suspect. The police found nothing. Despite his protests of innocence, he was hauled off to the new jail for questioning and incarcerated for nine days. Besides suffering the loss of his meager income from his day laboring, the family now had a reputation! Though charges were dropped for lack of evidence, he was now known as a "jailbird".

By February 11, 1858, Bernadette would have been regarded as one of the most pitiful children in all Lourdes. Stunted since the cholera attack, the fourteen-year-old girl looked about eleven. Her asthma would often have her clinging to the bars of the one window in the home, gasping for air. She often went hungry and still had never attended school.

However, there were things in her favor. She remained a cheerful soul, managed to keep clean and neat in her patched clothing and was very much loved and trusted by her parents and siblings. She had a good store of peasant toughness and common sense and strong trust in God. She could recite only the Our Father, Hail Mary and Creed, but that was enough for the Rosary. She loved to recite this prayer on the beads that were always in her pocket. She also slipped into the nearby parish church frequently to visit and talk with her Lord.

Suddenly God threw a beam of light onto this little nobody from the hovel. She would soon become Lourdes' most famous person, eventually loved by people all over the world. A Lady of unearthly beauty appeared to Bernadette, smiled and asked with a bow of respect, "Will you do me the favor of coming here for a fortnight?" The Lady honored the sickly young girl by using "*vous*" for "you", not the offhand "*tu*" that everyone else gave this inconsequential adolescent. A team of horses—in the persons of the public prosecutor, the chief of police, the parish priest, the nuns, some of her family and many townspeople—could not stop Bernadette from responding to that invitation. At the beginning of the fourth visit there was that cacophony of evil voices from the river screaming at Bernadette to "get out of here". With one authoritative glance from the Lady, the voices fled, and the Grotto was at peace again.

The first Sunday of Lent, a bone-chilling February 21, marked the sixth visit. That was the first time nonchurchgoing Dr. Dozous went to watch an apparition. Over drinks at his club the night before, he said he was sure the much-talked-about Bernadette was a neat case of neuropathy. He went along to prove it on February 21. He carefully watched, checked her pulse and breathing for pathological symptoms of catalepsy, but found absolutely none. However, he noticed how her expression changed during the apparition from ecstatic joy to great sadness, with tears flowing down her cheeks. After the vision finished the doctor asked her why: "She gazed into the distance over my head", replied Bernadette. "When she looked at me again, I asked her what was making her sad. She replied, 'Pray to God for sinners.'" This was the beginning of the Lady's messages about sin, conversion and suffering. Later that day Bernadette had to taste the first bitter interrogations from Prosecutor Dutour and Chief of Police Jacomet.

For the eighth apparition, Wednesday, February 24, four to five hundred came, according to the police estimate. During that vision Bernadette's face clouded over again, and she wept. Clasping her rosary tightly, she murmured half aloud, "Penance, penance, penance!"

Many now believed her, noting there was nothing in the messages that was not in the Gospels. The ninth apparition, on February 25, however, disillusioned most onlookers. That day Bernadette, having moved around apparently aimlessly on her knees, suddenly bent low and began digging in the dank frozen ground with her fingers. Muddy water seeped into the hole she made. She scooped up a handful, drank and smeared some over her face. "She's mad", came the voices of onlookers. Later Bernadette explained, "She told me to drink and wash at the spring she pointed to."

Most witnesses left in disgust and disbelief that day. Some stayed on, however, and were amazed to see water running from the small hole Bernadette had made. The flow gradually increased to a swift-flowing spring, now pouring out thousands of liters a day. Former quarry worker Louis Bouriette, blind in one eye from a blasting accident nineteen years before, had his daughter go and dip a cloth in the water. He prayed, applied it to his blind eye and saw. Dozous, his doctor, was dumbfounded—the cure was medically inexplicable. Dozous would eventually become a believer and Bernadette's stout ally.

On Saturday, February 27, eight hundred came to witness the tenth apparition. Word of Bernadette's small fingers starting a spring brought many of the doubters back. During her ecstasy she frequently bent low to kiss the cold and lifeless earth. Asked afterward why she did it, she said the Lady told her to do this as a penance for sinners.

The first three apparitions had been all smiles and sweetness, filling Bernadette with happiness and confidence. Then a penitential dimension entered. Mary's expression took on a deep sadness as she spoke to Bernadette of what sin does. She asked the little seer, and through her the onlookers, to pray and do penance for the conversion of people alienated from God. Luke 19:41 shows Jesus weeping over Jerusalem. Hebrews 5:7 tells us Jesus "offered up prayer and entreaty, aloud and in silent tears".

The Lourdes apparitions are replete with biblical symbols—the wilderness site under a mountain, the new spring, the humble listening, the drinking and washing. There is surely profound biblical symbolism, too, in Bernadette's kissing the earth. The Bible opens with Adam being made from the earth in Genesis 2:7. We who came from the earth, and live on food that springs from the earth, at death return to the earth. The Ash Wednesday liturgy reminds us dramatically that we come from clay and return to clay. Bernadette was asked to kiss the winter-hardened, dark and seemingly lifeless ground at the foot of the Grotto. It was a chaotic mix of soil and stone torn from the uplands during ancient storms and ground into the valley by ice-age glaciers. I think the Lady, in asking Bernadette to bend and kiss the earth, was asking her to accept lovingly—for that is what a kiss means—her human situation, the pain as well as the joy in her earthbound life. She was asked to embrace the here and now of her life as a member of a wounded humanity. Bernadette did the Lady's bidding and did it joyfully. In so doing she began to see meaning and beauty in her cholera-weakened and asthmatic body, in the squalor, humiliation and weakness of life in the Cachot. Mary had led Bernadette to the "blessedness" of Jesus' topsy-turvy Sermon on the Mount, where happy are those who mourn, who are poor, who are persecuted in the cause of right!

Bernadette rose up to become a magnificent woman. She continued to serve God and her fellows lovingly despite her asthmatic lungs, which often made her gasp for air. Some years later the then-prevalent TB of the bone—caries—slowly destroyed her body. She died at age thirty-five, by which time she was a heroic saint. Cinderella had become a princess, much beloved of the Crown Prince. Literally hundreds of fine writers have since published books on her life. Multitudes go every year to the convent in Nevers, where her incorrupt body is venerated in a glass coffin. Bernadette, who never let herself become dull or morose, had embraced life's harsh winters as well as its shining springs and fruitful autumns. She loved her parents despite their incompetence and at times stupidity. She suffered greatly in Lourdes, but in the Nevers convent spoke with great joy and nostalgia about the poplar-lined valleys of her childhood. She accepted the sadness of heart we all feel at times, understanding it as nostalgia for our true home, which is eternal life with God in the mystery of the beatific vision.

ABOVE: *Bernadette's body, exhumed for reburial thirty years and five months after her death, was incorrupt.*

BELOW: *The incorrupt body of Saint Bernadette lies in state, in Convent Chapel, Nevers, France.*

Most of the sick who go to Lourdes are not cured physically, but they have a strong desire to go there again despite the hardships of the journey. The attraction is the peace they find there, and the discovery of a meaning to their ailments. God is real and close. There often comes a new consciousness of his teaching in the Bible about this life being a journey, not a destination. Their illnesses and disappointments become "appointments" that lead to a deeper wisdom and an opportunity to help others who do not know God's love. Their sicknesses take on the nobility of a vocation, the call to participate in the mystery expressed by Paul in Colossians 1:24, "joyful to be suffering for you, making up in my own body what still remains to be undergone of Christ's sufferings for his body, the Church".

In 1224, two years before his death, Francis of Assisi was in emotional distress, fearing the great movement he had begun was disintegrating. He went off to rugged Mount Alverna and in imitation of his Lord spent forty days in prayer and fasting. As he meditated on Christ's Passion, he began to beg for two graces: To experience in his own body and soul Jesus' anguish on the Cross, and to experience, as far as humanly possible, the love that led his Lord to embrace such suffering for us. Heaven answered his pleas with the famous stigmata, wounds in his hands, feet and side. Despite his efforts to hide these wounds, his Franciscan brethren often saw them.

The spirit of the adolescent, fun-loving Francis had almost been crushed by defeat on a battlefield, imprisonment and a near-fatal sickness. Those experiences had occasioned his first wholehearted turning to Christ. Then he met a leper so repulsive that the temptation was to flee. But he rose above his loathing and fear and went and embraced the pitiful man. Now, years later in 1224, he received his greatest graces—to love like Christ, even loving the suffering that helps bring freedom and salvation to others.

Many balk and are embittered and demoralized by suffering. They sometimes lose faith or trust in God. How could a loving God allow such suffering? Francis solved that problem in contemplating God himself nailed to a cross. That cross became the mountain signpost for the rest of the journey home—a signpost rooted in the earth, pointing to God the Father, its arms flung wide, embracing all peoples. For Bernadette, the sadness on Mary's face led her to the mystery of the pain of God and his great desire to lead us home.

Suffering can become like the winter that allows the ground to wait and rest a while. It is meant to lead us to a deeper, stronger wisdom. An Arab proverb puts it like this: If it is all sunshine, the world will end up all desert. A seminal book— "a central work in the development of Japanese taste", wrote Japanologist Professor Donald Keene—is *Tsurezure-Gusa* (Essays in Idleness). Essay 117 in Keene's classic translation warns of seven kinds of people who will make unreliable friends. Number three is "the one of robust constitution who has never known a day's illness". It seems to be the commonsense wisdom of all cultures that the experience of suffering is necessary if we are to become people of strength, depth and reliability. A word that appeals to all of us is "compassion". It is derived from Latin words meaning "suffer" and "in company with".

There is a modern tendency in the West, abetted by our ever-present slick advertising and glossy magazines, to view suffering as evil. We are encouraged to fear it and flee from it as unnatural, and this can cause apprehension and mental stress that are major causes of "self-inflicted" sicknesses common among First World people—a people assured that this present life is the only life and that we have a right to be completely happy and fulfilled here below. Many feel cheated when they discover they are not gloriously happy! If death is viewed as a disaster, one can subconsciously hasten it precisely

Singing the "Ave" during evening procession, Lourdes.

because one resents and fears it! Many people certainly worry themselves sick. Francis, who loved life, sang joyfully of "Sister Death", the wise elder sister who would guide her little brother over the final twists on the road home to the Father. Bernadette said that if you have seen our Lady, nothing of earth could make your heart captive.

Alexis Carrel, after wandering forty years through endless deserts of agnosticism, began to pray and discovered something that satisfied him more than his scientific breakthroughs. His article "Prayer Is Power", in the April 1941 *Reader's Digest*, testified to "tranquillity . . . vigor, moral stamina, and . . . understanding" that come with a "habit of prayer". He continued, "As a physician I have seen men, after all other therapy has failed, lifted out of disease and melancholy by the serene effort of prayer. . . . We sadly underestimate prayer . . . [if we think it] a childish petition for material things . . .

[which is like] describing rain as something that fills the birdbath. . . . We derive most power from prayer as a supplication to become more like him." He concludes with a reference to World War II, which was then raging: "Today prayer is . . . a binding necessity. . . . The lack of emphasis on the religious sense has brought the world to the edge of destruction." Lourdes, where the adult Carrel first thought seriously about the supernatural, is above all a place of prayer, prayer that gives people a vision beyond material things and creates a yearning to "become more like him"—like the Christ who embraced our sufferings and death because they too are part of the journey home.

The 1960s saw the rise of the drug culture. Enthusiastic prophets said the new generation could be free. Reality, they assured us, was what you chose it to be. The new gospel of Woodstock proclaimed that if you want to you can create your own meaning and happiness. Cannabis and LSD were the new sacraments to heal pain and solve tensions. The London *Sunday Times* columnist Bryan Appleyard summed up the fruits: "Nihilism, solipsism and antithought". Solipsism assures us the only sure reality is our own thoughts. Postmodernism solemnly and sadly proclaims we cannot have certainty about anything. Lewis Carroll's *Alice in Wonderland* contains a kind of preview of this when Humpty Dumpty tells Alice that words have the meaning he chooses to give them. When Alice has a conversation with the mad Red King, she becomes fearful that nothing is real, all is a weird dream. She finds herself hoping that at least it is her own dream, that she has not been dreamed into existence by the mad Red King!

The doubt about everything promoted by the postmodernists is obvious in not a little modern religious writing. The Jesus Seminar people—who certainly do not doubt the importance of getting media coverage—prefer question marks to full stops after most Bible verses. God, the Resurrection, morality, life after death, prayer—they all eventually tumble like Humpty Dumpty. All the king's horses and all the king's men cannot bring it all together again—only a patient, merciful Author of the Bible can do that! Maybe as a student you took part in those debates in which you were given the subject, and the positive or negative side fifteen minutes before the start. It was good practice for thinking on your feet and also an illustration of how you can make a case for or against most things if you are nimble-minded. Yes, theories come cheaply—education theories, moral theories, social theories. History shows any number of Hitlers and Stalins whose theories, aided by skillful propaganda, brought disaster to millions. One fact, however, is more reliable than countless theories. Facts of healing at Lourdes, as with similar facts in Jesus' ministry, have helped countless millions make decisions about their lives. The other solid facts of peace of heart and new spiritual energy are confirmation of the authenticity of their decisions.

Episcopalian Bishop Phillips Brooks of Boston (1835–1893) wrote powerfully about prayer. His words are the kind of corrective we need in our soft-option, cheap-grace, anything-goes culture. The God he came to know was the Eagle-God often referred to in the Old Testament and incarnate in Jesus. We are called to become like him, eagles who do not fear mountain storms—and are rewarded with vista visions. The soft-option culture is turning out domesticated hens, which spend a lifetime grubbing for scraps on the ground. Any rotten scraps will do as long as they are pleasurable. Earth-bound hens' vision is confined to the ground in front of their beaks.

Here's a sample of Brooks on prayer: "Do not pray for easy lives. Pray to be stronger men. Do not pray for tasks equal to your powers. Pray for powers equal to your tasks. Then the doing of your work shall be no miracle, but you shall be a miracle. Every day you shall wonder at yourself, at the richness of life which has come to you by the Grace of God."

Tertullian, who died in 230 A.D., left similar advice: "Prayer possesses no special grace to avert the experiences of suffering, but it arms with endurance those who suffer, who grieve, who are in pain. It makes grace multiply in power so that faith may know what it obtains from the Lord, while it understands it is suffering for God's Name."

Pilgrims at the Lourdes Basilica.

Chapter 17

FIRE IN THE BELLY

A Challenge to Priests

THERE WAS AN ART EXHIBITION in Australian cities in 1998 called *Beyond Belief: Art and Religious Imagination*. Well-known art critic John McDonald made this comment on it: "Modern artists like modern poets have tried to give expression to a painful longing to believe coupled with an inability to believe." He then quoted the British poet C. H. Sisson:

> O crucifix . . .
> Silently but so loved you tear the sky.
> Wherefore those tears?
> Shall I rejoice?
> I would do so if I could hear your voice!

If you've read Augustine's *Confessions* you will remember he suffered anguish like that before he met Christ. There is much in that sophisticated, restless young fourth-century philosopher that puts one in mind of so many of our brilliant,

233

educated but often jaded young people. At eighteen he was keeping a mistress. He tried the religion of the Manicheans. It was upbeat and used upscale philosophical jargon, not unlike New Age in some ways. Nor was it demanding morally. But in the long run it left him dissatisfied and angry. It took a long struggle before he was ready to listen seriously to the Gospels. Augustine had to overcome two obstacles—fierce independence, coming from what he finally saw as intellectual pride, and his own sexual immorality. But he knew he was not really happy and eventually took the plunge of humbly listening to Ambrose explain the Christian faith. He was thirty-three when Ambrose baptized him. His *Confessions* had and still have the power of a man who has at last found God, himself and peace. "You have made us for yourself, O Lord, and our hearts are restless until they rest in thee", he wrote. Also, "Late have I loved thee, O Beauty ever ancient, O Beauty ever new." I don't know about C. H. Sisson, but many intellectuals today are adrift spiritually because like younger Augustine they are adrift morally. Pride and the sins of the flesh muddy the eyes of the soul.

However, there are other obstacles to belief, and we believers are responsible for some big ones. Nietzsche, the first to speak of "the death of God", once said he would take Christians more seriously if they looked more redeemed! Halfhearted believers are not likely to be go-betweens for God and genuine seekers. Rahner even said that moralizing preachers without love create atheists!

I have tried to present the healing miracles of Lourdes as strong reason why unbelievers might start seeking God in prayer. But the Lourdes messages are primarily for believers. They are a call to prayer of the heart and committed gospel living. They repeat what Christ said (Lk 12:49): "I have come to cast fire on the earth, and how I long for its blazing now!" Jesus, and Mary at Lourdes, manifested deep sadness at the state of our race. They are calling for people with—to use an apt expression—fire in their belly.

I had a problem in my early twenties with believing in Jesus' "loving Father" and in the Christian Church. Now I am seventy, and the media has the same problem. Many journalists see the Church as a ship breaking up irreparably under the pounding of huge seas and cyclonic winds. Without doubt, Christian belief is undergoing a tremendous crisis. As a priest-religious, I'd like to throw my hat into the widening ring of diagnoses.

We priests and religious have lost much prestige among Catholics, and non-Catholics, since I was ordained in 1953. While I was in Dublin during August of 1997, an Irish priest was convicted of pedophilia and given a lengthy sentence. As he was led from the courtroom, one of his victims shouted, "I hope you rot in hell!" At a parish Mass the following Sunday a priest said in his homily, "That was a very uncompassionate thing to say." A woman in the church immediately stood up and shouted, "What about compassion for the victims!" The congregation broke into spontaneous clapping. This was reported in the media, and over the next few days several commentators cited this as indicative of a new attitude in Ireland. Priests and religious used to be venerated. They had suffered with the people during the harsh colonial days and the long famine. People listened to and usually accepted what they said. No longer was this so. Priests and religious now had to prove themselves.

Father Michael Whelan, who has a doctorate in spirituality, recently spoke about the Australian Church scene. He noted the past prestige of priests and religious who usually had to struggle through hard days and scrimp personally to keep Catholic schools, hospitals and charities up and running. Now, however, the scene has changed dramatically. There appear the first signs of that resentment, noted earlier

concerning the anti-Catholic movements in France and Portugal, against special clerical privileges. Priests and religious
"have now to prove themselves in Australia too", he concluded.

Father Gerry Arbuckle has written seven books on bringing vitality back to shrinking congregations of vowed religious. The simple statistics of losses and shortage of entrants
indicate to him a crisis of terminal illness in many groups. He
notes especially morbid symptoms: the waning of committed
personal prayer, waning of mutual faith sharing about their
apostolate and failure to live the poverty they vowed.

Comments by two visiting Australian priests disturbed
me. I took notice of what they said, because they are missionaries who have done powerful work among the impoverished of the Third World. They stayed at a number of
Australian presbyteries and religious houses. The priest from
India remarked how in some "the drinks start earlier and the
television runs later, as does getting up in the morning.
Personal prayer time seems to be squeezed thin." The priest
from the Philippines spoke of "all the genuflecting before
the television set". When he was a youthful cleric in Australia, there was much more genuflecting in the chapel or
parish church by priests and religious going in to pray alone
with the Lord.

About ten years ago I stopped in the Philippines while
traveling back to Australia. I spent six days in the southern-
most island of Mindanao with a small group of missionaries,
mostly from New Zealand. None of the mission stations
possessed a television set or even a telephone. The priests
lived frugally. One rectory was in the middle of a squalid
slum. There were no beds or mattresses in the tiny rooms.
Like the slumdwellers around them, they lay down at night
on thin mats spread on the wooden floor. Despite their poor
living conditions, these priests were enthusiastic, full of spiri-

tual and human "get up and go". They had attracted quite a number of young men to their seminary, a simple, rented building. Some of their Filipino recruits were readying for ordination. They had more seminarians than their home provinces in New Zealand, Australia and England combined! Their poverty meant they had more time for visiting their people and a larger proportion of their money to buy medical help for the impoverished sick. Their parishioners began to imitate the latter action. Overseas acquaintances and people who heard about them began cutting down on luxuries so they could send monetary help to their medical work for impoverished Filipinos. My six days among them in the Philippines disturbed me in my material comfort, complacency—and spiritual ineffectiveness.

Another disturber-priest was William Johnston, a professor at Tokyo's Sophia University. He gave a retreat to a group of us priests working in Japan and startled us with this remark: "If you baptize adult Japanese without teaching them contemplation, you are irresponsible. No one can live the essential Christian charter, which is the Sermon on the Mount, without the strong love that comes in contemplation." He added, "Contemplation is available and essential to every adult who makes serious attempts. It can be as simple as the loving, regular and prayerful reading of Bible passages about God's concern for us."

Around the same time I heard lectures given by the saintly Scripture expert Carroll Stuhlmueller and designed especially for Christian preachers and teachers. Commenting on Psalm 63 he said, "We need long stretches of prayer to clear away distractions and 'feel' the helpless desperation we are in when we are without God . . . and to experience the necessary hunger for spiritual things. Only by such sustained prayer can our subconscious be plumbed and the 'vision' of God seen." If Stuhlmueller and Johnston were right, I had a long, long way to go. But I also had some answers, I thought, to the crisis of belief in the late twentieth century.

Recently I stayed with the very hospitable Franciscans at Roppongi, Tokyo. I came across letters Saint Francis of Assisi wrote about the spiritual crisis he saw in thirteenth-century Italy. He is surely one of the gentlest and most forgiving of mortals. However, he has some very tough and sobering words for those believers who presume on God's kindness and those religious who become casual about the gospel values to which they have committed themselves. The breviary readings during the same time, Easter Week, were from the Book of Revelation. They were addressed to some earlier Christian communities that had grown slack. The community of Sardis is told bluntly, "I know you are reputed to have life, but you are dead! Wake up! Bring life back to what you still have, lest it disappear completely!" The community at Laodicea must have been stunned by its special message: "You are neither hot nor cold . . . [but] lukewarm. I will cast you from my mouth. You say, 'I am rich, well provided with all I need!' You do not understand just how miserable, pitiful, poor, naked and blind you are!" (Rev 3).

I hear clear modern echoes of the Book of Revelation and of Francis in many pages of M. Scott Peck's *The Road Less Traveled*. Time and again the author writes of our potentially fatal inclination to drift, gradually relinquishing our precious ability to live responsibly and freely. He bluntly diagnoses this as inherent "laziness", inclining us to opt for the easy road. Though his book is full of tough and stern prescriptions, it was on the bestseller list in the United States for five years. This extraordinary bestseller phenomenon tells me that a great many people sense that our soft-option society is in deep crisis. They want to read books that tell the truth, unpalatable though this truth may seem at first. He has stern things to say about fellow psychiatrists who "use" patients, especially sexually. We Catholics have been rocked these last few years by the number of priests and religious who have done just that and betrayed people and Christ. The old advice went: It is dangerous to choose celibacy unless you are prepared to be a person of prayer, so that God becomes a real companion with whom you communicate at depth, daily.

Bernadette Soubirous died on April 16, 1879, of very painful tuberculosis of the bone. Thirty years later, on September 22, 1909, investigations began into possible declaration of her sainthood. Her coffin was opened, and her body was found to be incorrupt. Though her nun's habit was damp and her rosary rusted from the moisture in the casket, her remains were quite free of normal putrefaction or even bad odor. Japan's Yomiuri television did a documentary on Lourdes and Bernadette. It was in no way a Christian program, just a factual presentation for the 99 percent non-Christian Japanese. The narrator had done her homework well and led the audience from Lourdes into the Nevers chapel, where the body lies in a glass coffin. As she and the camera focused on Bernadette's serene and beautiful face, refined by her short lifetime of intense suffering, the narrator's voice choked, and she began to weep! In between sobs she struggled to ask, "Bernadette, what are you trying to tell us?"

I have been struggling for weeks to answer that question. I wrote this book mainly about miracles at Bernadette's Lourdes, in the hope of helping unbelievers or wobbly believers meet Jesus and the Father. I have distressing memories of many who came to see me over the years, seeking to know the meaning of life and death—and leaving unconvinced. I did not convince them, I know, because they did not meet the living Christ in me, did not see the loving servant-disciple that I solemnly vowed to be. A man who is a convert and who has held high government office recently touched a raw nerve in me—and exposed one reason for my failures to convince others—when he said, "Many priests are out for power." I thought of all the overriding of parishioners I've done, all the downright bullying of lay people when I could get away with it. I was very far from being the priest-disciple Jesus hoped for when he said, "I have come to serve, not to be served . . . I, the master, have washed your feet. You do likewise."

A May 1, 1999, letter in the *Tablet*, a British weekly, touched another raw nerve. Father David Maguire wrote, in response to articles about the falloff in Mass attendance and seminary enrollment, "Do people today see priests who are filled with passion to serve the gospel and their communities? . . . Are we as priests seen to be too comfortable in our presbyteries, too fond of nice cars, enjoying exotic holidays and so on? When I look on my own lifestyle I have to answer yes."

William Johnston, in the retreat he gave us priests, said you are a true Christian if you actually live by the Sermon on the Mount. Then he looked sharply at us! We guessed what he was thinking! A priest's one essential task is to live the Sermon on the Mount and help others to do likewise. If priests and religious and the people they vowed to serve are doing that, miracles of physical healing will not be all that important for helping unbelievers find the Father. Seekers will come to be sure he is real and loves them because they have heard his voice and experienced his love in Jesus' disciples.

Chesterton said that five times in history the Christian Church was on her deathbed. The miracle of resurrection took place only because committed saints led a radical renewal. I think we are witnessing the sixth serious illness of the Church—and of Western civilization, too, a civilization John Paul II describes as "the culture of death".

Vatican II was surely an initiative of the Holy Spirit in response to this modern crisis. It had a strong, simple message to priests and religious like me: Return to the spirit of your founders, people who lived the Sermon on the Mount.

Vatican II had a message for lay people too: *Semper reformanda est*, that is, "ever in need of reform", ever in need of sustained effort to live the gospel of love. This is precisely what Jesus said in his first preaching: Repent, and believe the good news (Mk 1:15). Lourdes, Knock and Fatima are simply a repeating of that message. All these apparitions were to lay people. After all, most people in the Church are lay people. Lay seers like Bernadette handed on the messages very faithfully.

Leading nineteenth-century secular-humanists had a rosy picture for the future. Through the irresistible advance of science, universal education and free trade, they prophesied, all major human problems would be solved in the twentieth century. They rejoiced to be living in the dawn. Their successors in the next century would live in the full light of the day!

But nineteenth-century nightmares, and worse, have persisted into our scientifically, educationally and commercially advanced times! I think Bernadette has proved to be a far better prophet than the scientific establishment that ridiculed her.

The blessing of the sick with the Eucharist, Lourdes.

Chapter 18

IMMACULATE CONCEPTION

The Triumph of Faith

I have written this book in the hope of helping some in their search to discover or rediscover the loving Creator. There is something more: The miracles at Lourdes and similar pilgrim shrines occur very often in the context of Christian sacraments—the Eucharist, reconciliation and the anointing of the sick—in other words, the Church. There is also, of course, the role of Mary.

I can sympathize with Protestants and some modern Catholics disturbed by deviation and superstition that have spoiled some Marian devotions. Once again it is the old problem of drifting off to an extreme—which has occurred on both sides! Later Protestants, for instance, went to extremes of denial that Luther did not teach. In his last sermon, January 17, 1546, just before his death, he preached, "Is Christ alone to be adored? Or is the holy Mother of God not to be honored? This is the woman who crushed the serpent's head. Hear us [Mary], for your Son denies you nothing." In a hymn he composed as a Protestant he sings: "She is my love, the noble Maid, Forget her I cannot. . . . My heart she has forever."

The miracles at Lourdes, Fatima and elsewhere have definitely taken place under Mary's "mantle". When she appeared to the seers she carried a Rosary, her special prayer, and urged its recitation. It was Mary who pointed out the place where Bernadette's fingers opened up a spring that has given God's gifts of physical and spiritual healing to many tens of thousands. God and his Christ do not mock us or confuse us with false signs. Mary is obviously more than a "superstitious accretion" in their plans.

Vatican II insisted that Marian devotion must be Christocentric, founded on solid doctrine. Some modern Catholics of obvious goodwill have overreacted by going to doctrinaire extremes. As Karl Rahner has insisted, we are not saved by bright ideas or ideologies! Some Catholic feminists, understandably reacting to extremes of patriarchalism, have dismissed Lourdes and Fatima because of Mary's "submissiveness". But Mary of Nazareth was very submissive to God, calling herself his *doule* (slave) in her Magnificat (Lk 1:48). Saint Paul calls himself the *doulos* of Christ in Romans 1:1 and Galatians 1:10. Paul further tells us in Philippians 2:7 that the Son of God "emptied himself to become a *doulos*". Paul and the Bible disciples lived with the creative tension of knowing they were beloved children of God but also *doulos* who owned absolutely nothing of themselves. Mary, possessing the faith and courage to accept and embrace these two poles, these two counterpoints of human existence, created the symphony of the Magnificat. She sings as the Valiant Woman, but without a single strident note.

Sri Lankan Father Balasuriya is rightly concerned about social justice and the cumbersome cultural baggage that Western missionaries brought to Asia. He seems to doubt the authenticity of Lourdes because the Lady did not highlight these, his present agenda. But maybe in God's timing, the year 1858, when the French Church was battling to uphold belief in Christ and the Gospels, sociological or missiological messages were not the critical ones. Lourdes had a profound effect on nineteenth-century French Catholicism. A century later French theologians would profoundly influence the sociology and missiology of Vatican II.

John Henry Newman, an expert on the first centuries of Christian theology, spoke of "development of doctrine" as one fundamental theological principle. A tree is truly in a seed and develops from it. Some seeds in the Gospels took centuries to develop and formulate—for instance, the understanding of the one Divine Person and two natures, divine and human, in Jesus. It took more than three centuries to decide the twenty-seven books of the New Testament.

Prayer to the saints and Mary, asking them to intercede with the Lord, came gradually. Beginning with Justin (converted circa 135, martyred circa 165), theologians began to speak of Mary as the New Eve. The first Eve, by disobedience, brought death. Mary, by obedience, cooperated with the New Adam in bringing the life of salvation. Irenaeus (martyred circa 193) expanded on this—Mary "by her obedience became to herself and the human race a cause of salvation. She untied the knot of disobedience." (Note: She was *a* cause of salvation, not *the* cause.) Epiphanius (died 403) called Mary "the mother of the living" and "associate of Jesus" in his saving work. The fourth- and fifth-century Western greats, Ambrose, Augustine and Jerome, and their contemporaries and equally famous Greeks, Chrysostom and Gregory of Nyssa, expanded on this theme of Mary as the New Eve and associate of Christ in his redeeming work.

The Roman baptism formula of the second century gives

Mary special mention. The Mass composed by Bishop Hippolytus about 215 does likewise. There is a famous papyrus fragment now kept in the John Rylands Museum, Manchester. Some experts date it to the fourth century. Papyrologist M. C. H. Roberts dates it to the late third century, as does expert in early Egyptian Christianity G. Giamberadini. The latter reconstructs this papyrus as follows: "Under your mercy we take refuge, Mother of God. Do not reject our supplications in necessity but deliver us from danger, [you] alone chaste, alone blessed." The first half of the Hail Mary prayer has been found on a potsherd dating from 600. A very famous and widely mentioned hymn of the Greek church is the *Akathistos*, dating from about 550. It sings to Mary as "the gate of heaven . . . who begets anew those who were [first] born in sin. . . . [You are the] receptacle of Divine Wisdom who shows how the philosophers lack wisdom while you enlighten the minds of faithful believers!"

Stories began to circulate among these early Christians of believers praying to Mary in times of trouble and being helped, often miraculously. One story that became especially famous was about Theophilus, a Greek cleric from Adana in Cilicia. The author, who claimed to be an eyewitness, put the events as happening in 538. This event gave birth to the Faust myth.

Cardinal Newman's robust devotion to Mary came with his lengthy study of the Church Fathers, those leading theologians of Christianity's early centuries. There are good books in English detailing Marian dimensions in the Fathers' spirituality. One excellent one is Hilda Graef's *Mary: A History of Doctrine and Devotion* (London: Sheed & Ward, 1963).

As already noted, Huysmans wrote *The Crowds of Lourdes* as a refutation of Zola's attack on Lourdes miracles. For that reason much of the book is devoted to cases of the instantaneous healing of physical diseases of long standing. However, he also wrote about forerunners of the Lourdes shrine. He discussed the healing shrines of Mary in two places not far from Lourdes, Garaison and Betharram. Both date from the early sixteenth century and were destroyed in the anti-Christian violence of the late eighteenth-century French Revolution—as the similar shrine at Walsingham, Norfolk (dating from 1061), was destroyed in 1538 on Henry VIII's orders. In Huysman's own nineteenth-century France there were the Paris Marian shrines of the Miraculous Medal at Rue du Bac (1830) and Our Lady of Victories (1836) and La Salette (1846) in southeastern France.

One of Catholicism's many struggles to define its doctrine, and a classical example of Newman's "development from a seed", is that concerning Mary's Immaculate Conception. Early Church Fathers wrote of her unique holiness and "sinlessness". For instance, Augustine, in *Concerning Nature and Grace* (published 415), said, "All men are sinners except the holy Virgin about whom, for the honor of the Lord, I want there to be no question of mentioning sin." However, this did not necessarily mean Mary was free from original sin. Christ redeemed the whole human race, which includes Mary. If she was not conceived, like everyone else, under the burden of original sin, how could Christ be her Redeemer? Thomas Aquinas, while teaching that she never sinned, taught that she inherited original sin at her conception. However, Duns Scotus, a Franciscan who taught at Oxford and died in 1308, made a theological distinction: Mary was free from original sin at the moment of her conception in her mother's womb "because of the foreseen saving work of Christ". Many who had a deep down sense of Mary's utter sinlessness because she was the unique Mother of the Savior quickly sensed the correctness of this theological opinion. The Dominicans, loyal to their great master Aquinas, were in opposition, an opposition that gradually disappeared because of the *sensus fidelium*, the spiritual intuition that developed in most Western Catholics, including the Dominicans.

Mary's apparitions to Saint Catherine Labouré in 1830, and the consequent wearing of the Miraculous Medal by millions almost overnight, gave great impetus to devotion to Mary's Immaculate Conception. The latter was a centerpiece of the medal that was given the name "miraculous" because of the extraordinary number of miracles claimed by wearers.

Pius IX, when he became Pope, chose twenty prominent theologians to discuss whether Mary's Immaculate Conception was an integral part of Catholic doctrine. They voted it was, seventeen to three. Next, on February 2, 1849, he sent an encyclical letter to all bishops in communion with Rome. They were to consult the theologians and the faithful in their dioceses. Should the Immaculate Conception be defined as Catholic doctrine? A total of 603 bishops answered yes, and 56 said no. Many of these "no" votes came from Protestant lands where Catholics were discriminated against. Bishops there thought a public declaration by the Pope might worsen Catholics' precarious position as mistrusted or hated minorities.

On December 8, 1854, Pius IX defined as part of the Church's faith that Mary, "in consideration of the merits of Jesus Christ, Savior of the human race, was preserved from the stain of original sin".

This was the period when the new science books were replacing the Bible among many intellectuals and national leaders. Mechanistic evolution was replacing Divine Providence. Charles Lyall, pointing to calcium remains from sea creatures that produced the White Cliffs of Dover, was explaining the gradual evolution of the world's surface. Charles Darwin, advancing the evidence he catalogued as a naturalist on the long voyage of H.M.S. *Beagle*, extended the theory of evolution to all animal life. Thomas Huxley concluded that man definitely descended from animals. Then he coined the new word "agnostic" ("not knowing"), calling all "Christian dogma" into question. For scientists this was the heady era of belief in unstoppable human progress. This new dogma replaced all God-dependent Christian ones. Churchmen taking on Thomas Huxley in debate were coming off a resounding second best. The tide of public opinion was with the atheists and agnostics.

François Voltaire, 1694–1778, had cried out with vehemence, "Crush the accursed thing", meaning the Christian Church. The French Revolution, beginning in 1789, attempted just that. As part of its program to de-Christianize the nation, Sunday was abolished; churches were turned into meeting halls and shops; and a new name was given to Notre Dame Cathedral, "Temple of Reason". To further mock the Virgin in whose name the cathedral was built in the eleventh century, a woman by the name of Maillard was brought in and proclaimed "Goddess of Reason".

In 1835 David Strauss brought out his *Leben Jesu* (Life of Jesus), debunking everything supernatural in the Gospels, miracles included, of course. Jesus was only a man, a mortal essentially the same as us. Ex-seminarian Joseph Renan came onto the French scene a little later, affirming that the only life left in the Church was that of perfume lingering on an emptied flower vase. "A [Christian] miracle", he said, "has no place in human affairs."

These were some of the many manifestations of the new culture, the new "religion", secular humanism. Christopher Dawson, in his *Progress and Religion*, wrote that "belief in the inevitability of progress" became the new alternative in Europe to the old Christian culture.[1] The new gospel was "Dawnism"—the belief that the nineteenth century was the

[1] Christopher Dawson, *Progress and Religion* (1929; reprint, Peru, Ill.: Sherwood, Sugden & Co., 1992).

dawn of a wonderful new era of light. Science, universal education and free trade would solve all major human problems. Christianity, with its crass submissiveness to the "pale Galilean" and its obsession about sin and guilt, was the great enemy of the promised progress.

When Pius IX proclaimed the Immaculate Conception of the Virgin, the new secularists laughed him to scorn. One hostile commentator called the Pope's definition "a triumph of irrationality".

For me there is a message in the timing of the Lourdes apparitions. Less than four years after the Pope's proclamation, "the Lady" appeared to Bernadette. Bernadette asked her several times who she was. During the sixteenth apparition, Thursday, March 25 (feast of the Annunciation, the conception of Christ in Mary's womb), she answered Bernadette. Joining her hands close to her breast, she raised her eyes to heaven and said, "I am the Immaculate Conception." Then, Bernadette said, Mary smiled and disappeared.

The sophisticated newspapers in Paris reported all this with mockery. But the healings began. Catherine Latapie, thirty-nine, was instantly healed of traumatic brachial palsy. Quarry worker Louis Bouriette, fifty-four, was cured of total blindness in the right eye. The eye had been sightless for nineteen years following a blasting accident. This was the miracle that first staggered local Dr. Dozous. He began attending Bernadette's apparitions sedulously, witnessed more miracles, became her defender and later wrote an invaluable book about the seer and Lourdes. The book was to make a powerful impression in France and beyond. The rationalists had challenged Gospel claims of miracles and supernatural revelation. Now an ex-rationalist was proclaiming God's response. Miracles as extraordinary as those in the Gospels were happening under the noses of scientists, especially French scientists, who were in the forefront of the attacks on the supernatural. God's response, it seems clear to me, was also confirmation of the Gospel's commissioning of Peter as chief shepherd and holder of the keys. Popes, like the rest of us have to "seek the Lord" daily, have to struggle to understand, cope, decide and, through it all, remain virtuous. Plenty of Popes have made plenty of mistakes and worse throughout history. There have been times when there were rival papal claimants and saints opting for different sides in the confusion. The first Pope, Simon Peter, fell badly. He was once severely put down by Jesus: "Get behind me, Satan! You are not thinking God's thoughts but human thoughts" (Mt 16:23). Yet despite all the human failures in Peter and his successors, the Last Supper prayer of Christ has been fulfilled: "Simon, Satan has desired to sift you all as wheat, but I have prayed for you, Simon, that your faith may not fail. Once you have turned back, you must strengthen your brethren." Despite all the personal failures, scandals and blunders, the Popes have preserved the essentials of the gospel, the belief in Christ as Divine Son sent by the Father, the Scriptures as God's word and the sacraments. Lourdes, for me, confirms these matters. Rome is called the Eternal City and has preserved the eternal truths. That is the supernatural dimension of the human papacy.

Invalids on stretchers.

AFTERWORD

THE ENGLISH POET Francis Thompson has a special message for modern youths. His father was a Manchester doctor, and Francis went to university to study medicine. He fought with his father, dropped out of medical school and became hooked on drugs. He ended up destitute, living on the streets of London, craving only opium. First an evangelical minister and then Wilfred and Alice Meynell helped him, very compassionately, face reality. He broke free of his addiction and became a recognized poet, leaving some enduring verse. You may have read his *Hound of Heaven*. Another of his fine poems is *In No Strange Land*. One stanza goes:

> The angels keep their ancient places—
> Turn but a stone and start a wing!
> 'Tis ye, 'tis your estranged faces
> That miss the many splendour'd thing.

What you find depends on what you are really looking for. There are those lines someone wrote about the two men "looking out through prison bars. One saw mud; the other saw stars." In the first chapter I mentioned Dr. West's book that debunked Lourdes miracles. L. Sabourin in his response, *Divine Miracles Discussed and Defended* (Rome: Officium Libri Catholici, 1977), pointed out that Dr. West never met any of the eleven Lourdes cases he wrote about.

Bernadette was once interviewed by a man who, having heard her testimony, replied, "I don't believe you." She responded, "My responsibility is to tell you what I saw, not to make you believe." Stanley Jaki remarked, "[Lourdes] miracles are never coercive. . . . A dispensation that is truly divine would never take away man's freedom." Spouses cannot be coerced into loving fidelity—that must always be a freely chosen thing.

The paleontologist and keen scientist Teilhard de Chardin said in his study *Lourdes Miracles and the Canonical Enquiries* (*Etudes* 118, 1909) that the unbiased inquirer will find at Lourdes "naked and objective reality". Karl Rahner was always a vigorous thinker very conscious of the need to base his beliefs on objective reality. He was no sentimentalist who based his philosophy and theology on mere emotion. However, he knew that beliefs that do not lead to an experience of love, our own and God's, are barren things. In his study *Visions and Revelations* he wrote of how genuine apparitions "deeply move the People of God, causing a response of enthusiasm for the message given. . . . They are touched by the sign of God's love and concern for them and his willingness to use stimulating means of awakening their response" (quoted in the Australian Jesuit magazine *Messenger*, July 1984).

While at Lourdes in 1997, I ran into a friend, Father John Burger, an American Columban missionary from Japan. When he heard I was researching miracles, he told me of a family friend who had received a miracle cure. He gave me Robert Gutherman's address in the United States. I wrote to him, and this is, briefly, his story. He was fourteen years old in February 1974, when he developed a terribly severe earache. A specialist gave him medication and performed a minor ear operation. The problem persisted. He was hospitalized in Saint Christopher's Hospital, Philadelphia. They found that infection had invaded bones in his ear. On March 7, 1974, doctors performed a matoidectomy—having found two bones and several nerves totally destroyed and the infection about to enter the brain. Dr. Turty informed the mother her son would be permanently deaf in that ear. Two "repair work" operations were still needed, but these could not restore the hearing.

Robert's mother and family began praying to a saintly American nun who had died in 1955. This Mother Katharine Drexel had established a convent a mile from their home. Mrs. Gutherman asked Mother Katharine, "As you would a good neighbor in times of trial" to help them, reminding her, too, that Robert had often been an altar server in a chapel Mother Katharine had built.

Robert was lying asleep in his ward, his good ear on his pillow, the bad ear covered in bandages. Someone in the corridor called his name, Bobby. He heard it clearly. The mother told the doctor her son was hearing with the bad ear. "Impossible", he replied. "Two vital bones have been destroyed." The doctor did not investigate. Robert was released from the hospital on March 13. A week later Dr. Turty did a quick check on the postoperation wound and told the mother to bring the boy back for a thorough examination on April 1. The mother did, and the doctor was "absolutely amazed". After the thorough examination, Dr. Turty said, "I don't believe it. He is actually reconstructing anatomy!" He explained that "the flesh was fusing together to repair the hole in the eardrum". Giving the boy a hearing test, he announced that hearing had been restored. He wrote on the boy's record

sheet, "Child reconstructing anatomy. Could this be possible?" On September 23, 1974, Robert had his final check.
His ear and hearing were perfectly normal. Robert wrote all
this to me on October 27, 1997, from his home in Croydon,
Pennsylvania, in a six-page letter. There has been no hearing
relapse. Other doctors have checked Dr. Turty's data and
declared the case medically inexplicable.

A little background on Mother Drexel, canonized October
1, 2000: She was the granddaughter of the founder of a
successful Philadelphia banking house. Katharine was educated by private governesses and as a young woman traveled
extensively across the United States and Europe. She was very
active on the Philadelphia social scene, and her vivacity,
intelligence (and money!) caught the eye of many a beau.
However, there was a restlessness in her—she was distressed
above all by the injustices suffered by Native Americans and
African Americans. On a trip to Europe in the 1880s, she
had an audience with the social reformer Pope Leo XIII. She
had decided she must give a large donation to a religious
order that would help these oppressed peoples. Which order
would use the money most effectively? The Pope surprised
her by suggesting that she start such an order! Katharine
Drexel did just that. She returned to the United States,
completed a novitiate with the Sisters of Mercy in Philadelphia and in 1891, with a few companions, founded the
Blessed Sacrament Sisters for Indians and Colored People. By
1935 she had established forty-nine houses—including a
school in Harlem and Xavier University in New Orleans for
Indians and African Americans. She spent her whole patri-
mony, $12 million, on this work. This was the woman Bobby
Gutherman's mother regarded as a heroine of love and a saint.

I spent eleven days at Fatima in 1997 and met some
impressive people who have made a life study of its history.
One was Father John de Marchi, who has lived there since

1943. His classic *Fatima from the Beginning* has come out in many languages. The English edition is in its tenth printing. He was a close friend of many of the 1917 witnesses, including the principal seer, Lucia.

He was eighty-three when I met him but retained almost youthful exuberance and mental sharpness. His life had seen plenty of action—setting up his Missionary Institute in Portugal, the United States, Ethiopia and Kenya and founding a periodical, *The Rainbow*. One Fatima happening that especially moved him occurred in the summer of 1946. A huge crowd had gathered, as is usual for the vigil of the thirteenth day of the month. The church confessionals had long lines waiting. He was asked early in the evening to help and began hearing confessions in a field not far from the basilica. It was just before 2 A.M. when the last penitent finished his confession. The priest walked back with him to the basilica, where Holy Hours were in progress. "You seem very tired", remarked Father de Marchi. "Yes, my wife and I have walked eight days to get here."

"Eight days? Why?"

"Padre, our little daughter was born blind. The doctors said she could never see. We decided to pray to Our Lady of Fatima for nine days, promising her we would walk on pilgrimage to her shrine if our little one was cured. Each night after our prayers we put drops of Fatima water in her eyes. On the last of the nine days, when we weren't even thinking about it, I passed by our child. The tiny one turned her face and followed me with her eyes! I nearly lost my head and shouted to my wife, 'Marie, come quick. She is seeing!'

"We waited several days before setting out for Fatima so that we could arrive for the vigil tonight and the celebration tomorrow."

"Where did you come from?" the priest asked. "From Tras-os-Montes, up north of Mogadouro", he replied. The priest knew the area. It was a good 125 miles distant as the crow flies. "That was a long journey by foot, friend."

"Yes," replied the young man, "but people all along the way were very kind. We had a place to sleep almost very night. Only once did we spend a night in the open, outside Leiria."

"What did you do for food?"

"We carried a supply of barley bread. That was sufficient."

The pair had now reached the basilica, and a young woman carrying a baby moved over to them. The man introduced Marie, his wife. "I was deeply moved", said Father de Marchi, "and put my hand on the head of the *miraculada* (cured one). Two jet-black eyes shone from under a sort of hood, and a little hand stretched out and pulled my beard. All three of us had tears in our eyes."

The priest forgot the weariness that had overcome him from hearing confessions through the night. He went to join in the next Holy Hour in the basilica—"I was no longer in Fatima. I was in Nazareth, Bethlehem, Jerusalem. Even more, I was in a corner of paradise."

The young couple were poor peasants. They would have neither the money nor the time to go through all the medical procedures to have the cure examined. That would take a number of years. But they had no need for anyone to assure them it was God's work. He loved them and their child. It was as simple as that! Because this kind of thing keeps happening, the crowds of pilgrims—many who walk on pilgrimage for several days—keep coming. For October 13, 1997, the year I was there, nine hundred thousand were present at the Mass celebrated in the huge plaza in front of the basilica. I did not hear of any physical miracles, but I am sure there were the more important ones, people finding or refinding God, and the peace that discovery brings.

ACKNOWLEDGMENTS

LOURDES
François Vayne, editor, *Lourdes Magazine*, for information and
    photographs.
Father John Poole, O.M.I.
Thérèse Franque, archivist
Journalist Christine Bray
Barry and Nicole Griffin
Dr. Michael Lasalle
Sister Mary Patrick
Sister Mary Noel
Ann Judson

FATIMA
Armando Mendes
Dominican Sisters
Bob Nesnick

PARIS
Wendy Rowe
Elizabeth Nienaltowska
Marist Fathers

UNITED KINGDOM
Dom Philip Jebb
Dom Francis Little
Dom Sebastian Moore
Community of Downside Abbey
Clive Birch, S.M.

IRELAND
Marion and James Carroll
Peader Clarke
Father Aidan Carroll
Monsignor Dominic Grealy
Marist community—Fathers Brian Keenan, Brendan Morrissey, Jim
    McElroy, Donal Kerr, Michael Maher
Mary Donahy

UNITED STATES
  Robert Gutherman
  Carl Quick

AUSTRALIA
  Dr. Padraic and Mary Grattan-Smith
  Dr. Padraic J. and Michele Grattan-Smith
  Marists—Fathers James Carty, Peter McMurrich, John Glynn, Aidan
    Carvill, Barry Miller, and Brother Michael Naughtin
  Bill Giles
  Roma O'Donnell
  Joan Gortley
  Lucia de Vries
  Frank Donovan
  Dot O'Donnell
  Rosie Payne
  Dorothy Thomas
  Tom Gillespie
  Bill and Dot Dougherty
  Matt and Ellen Dougherty
  Mary-Jane Silver
  Brenda Dowling